ITALIAN
COOKING

ITALIAN COOKING

General Editor
MARIA SCARLATTI

LANGHAM PRESS

CONTENTS

First published 1983 by Langham Press,
Langham Park, Catteshall Lane, Godalming,
Surrey

In association with Octopus Books Limited,
59 Grosvenor Street,
London W1.

© Octopus Books Limited 1983

ISBN 0 86362 012 4

Produced by Mandarin Publishers Ltd
22a Westlands Road, Quarry Bay, Hong Kong

Printed in Hong Kong

INTRODUCTION

Italian cooking is popular the world over, but to many people it does not mean much more than pasta, pizza and ice cream. How surprised they would be to find the enormous choice of dishes and regional variety available in Italy. A quick look back into history will supply the answer. Before 1861 Italy was a collection of autonomous states, each with its own customs and traditions and, above all, its style of cooking. These differences are very much in evidence today and each region prides itself on its local specialities.

The North of Italy has traditionally been the richest area with the best soil and here cream, butter, fresh meat and pasta are staples. In the arid South, where the people have had to scratch an existence from the soil, the food is hotter and much use is made of garlic, herbs and olive oil.

Some foods are eaten throughout Italy, such as pasta and sausages, both of which are said to have been brought back from China by Marco Polo. But even these will vary from place to place. Throughout their tumultuous history the Italians have made the most of whatever ingredients are available, and produced the most delicious results.

A meal in Italy starts with antipasti or a soup, followed by pasta, then a main course of meat, fish, or game with vegetables or a salad and finally the meal ends with fresh fruit, ice cream or a dessert. Wine is the natural accompaniment and every region produces its own.

When cooking Italian food at home, there are some tips which, if followed, will make the results much more authentic. Italians like their pasta and their vegetables to be cooked *al dente* – literally, to the teeth – which means they should still have a little bite in them. Olive oil and fresh herbs should be used whenever possible and salad dressings should be made with wine vinegar or lemon juice.

Recipes in this book include metric, imperial and American measurements. Please use one set of instructions only, as they are not interchangeable.

BAGNO CALDO

METRIC/IMPERIAL	AMERICAN
2 carrots	2 carrots
2 celery sticks	2 celery stalks
1 bulb fennel	1 bulb fennel
1 red pepper, halved and seeded	1 red pepper, halved and seeded
1 green pepper, halved and seeded	1 green pepper, halved and seeded
1 bunch spring onions	1 bunch scallions
100 g/4 oz mushrooms	1 cup mushrooms
bread sticks	bread sticks
Dip:	Dip:
6 cloves garlic, crushed	6 cloves garlic, crushed
6 anchovy fillets, mashed	6 anchovy fillets, mashed
6 × 15 ml spoons/6 tablespoons olive oil	6 tablespoons olive oil
75 g/3 oz butter	6 tablespoons butter

Prepare the vegetables and cut into strips or pieces. Leave the mushrooms whole, or cut into quarters if large.

To prepare the dip: mash the garlic and anchovy fillets to a paste in a small pan. Gradually stir in the oil. Add the butter and place over low heat for about 10 minutes, stirring occasionally. Transfer the pan to a spirit stove if available, and surround with vegetables and bread sticks. Serve immediately.
SERVES 4

ANTIPASTI

METRIC/IMPERIAL	AMERICAN
1 × 50 g/1¾ oz can anchovies	1 × 2 oz can anchovies
1 × 198 g/7 oz can tuna	1 × 7 oz can tuna
175 g/6 oz peeled prawns	1 cup shelled shrimp
1 × 120 g/4¼ oz can sardines	1 × 4¼ oz can sardines
100 g/4 oz Mortadella sausage, sliced	¼ lb Mortadella sausage, sliced
100 g/4 oz salami, thinly sliced	¼ lb salami, thinly sliced
3 hard-boiled eggs, quartered	3 hard-cooked eggs, quartered
½ cucumber, sliced	½ cucumber, sliced
3 tomatoes, quartered	3 tomatoes, quartered
1 × 400 g/14 oz can artichoke hearts	1 × 16 oz can artichoke hearts
lettuce	bibb lettuce
olive oil	olive oil
wine vinegar	wine vinegar

Arrange these foods, or a selection, on plates. Pour over a little oil and vinegar and serve immediately.
SERVES 4 TO 6

Bagno Caldo; Fondue

FONDUE

METRIC/IMPERIAL
175 g/6 oz Fontina cheese,
  rind removed and cut into
  thin slices
milk for soaking
2 egg yolks, lightly beaten
15 g/½ oz butter
salt
freshly ground white pepper
grated nutmeg (optional)
To garnish:
few thin slices of white bread,
  cut into small triangles and
  toasted
1 small white truffle, very
  thinly sliced (optional)

AMERICAN
6 oz Fontina cheese, rind
  removed and cut into thin
  slices
milk for soaking
2 egg yolks, lightly beaten
1 tablespoon butter
salt
freshly ground white pepper
grated nutmeg (optional)
To garnish:
few thin slices of white bread,
  cut into small triangles and
  toasted
1 small white truffle, very
  thinly sliced (optional)

Put the cheese slices into a bowl, cover with milk and leave to soak for 4 to 6 hours. Drain the cheese, reserving the milk. Put the cheese into the top of a double boiler or a basin over a pan of water. Add 2 × 15 ml spoons/2 tablespoons of the milk, the egg yolks, butter, salt, pepper and nutmeg to taste.

Cook over gently simmering water, stirring frequently, until the ingredients melt into a thick, smooth cream. Pour immediately into individual soup bowls and stand triangles of toast around the edge. If using the truffle, sprinkle the slices over the surface. Serve immediately.
SERVES 2

ARTICHOKE SALAD

METRIC/IMPERIAL
1 lettuce, shredded
1 × 400 g/14 oz can artichoke
  hearts, drained
100 g/4 oz Mortadella
  sausage, sliced
black olives
Dressing:
4 × 15 ml spoons/4
  tablespoons olive oil
3 × 15 ml spoons/3
  tablespoons lemon juice
1 clove garlic, crushed
salt
freshly ground black pepper

AMERICAN
1 bibb lettuce, shredded
1 × 16 oz can artichoke
  hearts, drained
¼ lb Mortadella sausage,
  sliced
ripe olives
Dressing:
¼ cup olive oil
3 tablespoons lemon juice
1 clove garlic, crushed
salt
freshly ground black pepper

Arrange the lettuce on 4 plates. Place the artichoke hearts, Mortadella and olives on the lettuce.

Whisk the dressing ingredients together in a bowl. Pour the dressing over the salad and serve immediately.
SERVES 4

CHICKEN LIVER TOASTS

METRIC/IMPERIAL	AMERICAN
40 g/1½ oz butter, plus extra for shallow frying	3 tablespoons butter, plus extra for shallow frying
1 small shallot, finely chopped	1 small shallot, finely chopped
3 – 4 fresh sage leaves	3 – 4 fresh sage leaves
225 g/8 oz chicken livers, cleaned and finely chopped	½ lb chicken livers, cleaned and finely chopped
freshly ground black pepper	freshly ground black pepper
8 pieces bread, 5 mm/¼ inch thick, cut into triangles	8 pieces bread, ¼ inch thick, cut into triangles
1 × 5 ml spoon/1 teaspoon lemon juice	1 teaspoon lemon juice
1 × 15 ml spoon/1 tablespoon chopped parsley to garnish	1 tablespoon chopped parsley to garnish

Melt 40 g/1½ oz (3 tablespoons butter) in a small saucepan and gently sauté the shallot and sage leaves together for about 5 minutes. Discard the sage leaves.

Add the chicken livers and pepper and cook gently, stirring frequently for about 6 minutes, or until the livers are no longer pink. Meanwhile, fry the pieces of bread in the extra butter until crisp and golden on both sides. Drain on kitchen paper towels. Stir the lemon juice into the liver mixture and adjust the seasoning. Spread the chicken liver mixture over the croûtes and sprinkle with parsley. Serve immediately.

SERVES 4

FLORENTINE TARTLETS

METRIC/IMPERIAL	AMERICAN
Pastry:	Dough:
225 g/8 oz plain flour	2 cups all-purpose flour
salt	salt
100 g/4 oz margarine	½ cup margarine
water	water
Filling:	Filling:
8 streaky bacon rashers, rinds removed and finely chopped	8 fatty bacon slices, rinds removed and finely chopped
100 g/4 oz packet frozen chopped spinach, thawed	¼ lb packet frozen chopped spinach, thawed
100 g/4 oz grated Parmesan cheese	1 cup grated Parmesan cheese
3 eggs	3 eggs
6 × 15 ml spoons/6 tablespoons milk	6 tablespoons milk
salt	salt
freshly ground black pepper	freshly ground black pepper

Sieve the flour and salt into a bowl and rub (cut) in the margarine. Add enough water to make a stiff dough. Roll our the dough thinly and cut into rounds, using a 7.5 cm/3 inch cutter. Use the round to line 30 patty tins.

Put the bacon in a small saucepan. Sauté over a moderate heat for 1 minute. Add the spinach and cook for a further 1 minute. Allow to cool. Arrange the spinach mixture in the lined patty tins and top with the grated cheese. Beat the eggs, milk and salt and pepper together and carefully pour into pastry (dough) cases.

Place in a preheated hot oven (220°C/425°F, Gas Mark 7) and cook for about 15 minutes. Serve warm.

MAKES ABOUT 30

PARMA HAM WITH MELON

METRIC/IMPERIAL	AMERICAN
1 ripe melon	1 ripe melon
6 – 8 thin slices Parma ham	6 – 8 thin slices Parma ham

Chill the melon for 1 hour in the refrigerator. Cut the melon into 6 or 8 slices and remove the seeds. Place a portion of melon on each of 6 or 8 individual serving plates. Drape a slice of ham over each piece of melon. Serve immediately. As an alternative, Parma ham can also be served with figs.

SERVES 6 TO 8

RISOTTO MILANESE

METRIC/IMPERIAL	AMERICAN
50 g/2 oz butter	¼ cup butter
1 small onion, finely chopped	1 small onion, finely chopped
25 g/1 oz beef marrow (optional)	1 oz beef marrow (optional)
350 g/12 oz Italian rice	2 cups Italian rice
4 × 15 ml spoons/4 tablespoons white wine	¼ cup white wine
1.2 litres/2 pints hot chicken stock	5 cups hot chicken bouillon
½ × 2.5 ml spoon/¼ teaspoon powdered saffron (optional)	¼ teaspoon powdered saffron (optional)
2 × 15 ml spoons/2 tablespoons grated Parmesan cheese	2 tablespoons grated Parmesan cheese
salt	salt
freshly ground black pepper	freshly ground black pepper
grated Parmesan cheese to serve	grated Parmesan cheese to serve

Melt 25 g/1 oz (2 tablespoons) of the butter in a heavy based saucepan and sauté the onion gently for 7 minutes until golden. Add the marrow, if using, and the rice and stir until the rice is translucent. Add the wine and cook until almost completely absorbed. Then begin stirring in the hot stock (bouillon), a little at a time, adding more as soon as the previous addition is almost absorbed. Stir frequently, and cook uncovered over a moderate heat.

Towards the end of the cooking add the saffron, if using, dissolved in 1 × 15 ml spoon/1 tablespoon of the hot stock (bouillon). Stir in the remaining butter, the Parmesan cheese and salt and pepper to taste.

The risotto is ready when the rice is tender but firm and the consistency is creamy. Serve immediately, with extra Parmesan cheese.

SERVES 6

Parma Ham with Melon

RISOTTO SCAMPI

METRIC/IMPERIAL	AMERICAN
450 g/1 lb green prawns	1 lb green jumbo shrimp
1.2 litres/2 pints water	5 cups water
1 fish head or small, whole fish	1 fish head or small, whole fish
1 celery stick, sliced	1 celery stalk, sliced
1 small onion, sliced	1 small onion, sliced
1 small carrot, sliced	1 small carrot, sliced
1 bay leaf	1 bay leaf
salt	salt
freshly ground black pepper	freshly ground black pepper
75 g/3 oz butter	6 tablespoons butter
2 × 15 ml spoons/2 tablespoons olive oil	2 tablespoons olive oil
1 clove garlic, crushed	1 clove garlic, crushed
200 g/7 oz raw, short-grain rice (Italian Arborio)	1 cup raw, short-grain rice (Italian Arborio)
good pinch each of ground cinnamon, nutmeg and cloves	good pinch each of ground cinnamon, nutmeg and cloves
1 × 15 ml spoon/1 tablespoon finely chopped parsley	1 tablespoon finely chopped parsley
3 × 15 ml spoons/3 tablespoons freshly grated Parmesan cheese	3 tablespoons freshly grated Parmesan cheese

If the prawns are still in their shells, peel (shell), devein and place the shells and heads in a large saucepan with the water, fish head or whole fish, celery, onion, carrot, bay leaf and salt and pepper to taste. Bring to the boil, simmer for 30 minutes, then strain into a measuring jug.

Put 65 g/2½ oz/5 tablespoons of the butter and the oil in a wide, heavy saucepan or deep frying pan (skillet) and heat. Add the garlic and sauté over a medium heat for 1–2 minutes, then add the rice and stir until golden. Add 250 ml/8 fl oz/1 cup reserved fish stock (bouillon), cover the pot, and simmer for 10 minutes or until liquid is absorbed. Add another 600 ml/1 pint (2½ cups) stock (bouillon) and simmer, covered, for a further 10 minutes. Add the raw prawns and continue cooking, covered, for 5–6 minutes longer or until the prawns are pink and the stock (bouillon) absorbed. Gently stir in the spices, remaining butter, parsley and cheese. Taste for seasoning and serve immediately on heated plates.
SERVES 4

Risotto Scampi

RISOTTO MARINARA

METRIC/IMPERIAL	AMERICAN
2 × 15 ml spoons/2 tablespoons olive oil	2 tablespoons olive oil
2 cloves garlic, crushed	2 cloves garlic, crushed
100 g/4 oz long grain rice	½ cup long grain rice
1 × 250 g/9 oz can baby clams, drained	1 × 9 oz can baby clams, drained
1 × 250 g/9 oz can mussels in brine, drained	1 × 9 oz can mussels in brine, drained
300 ml/½ pint fish or chicken stock	1¼ cups fish or chicken bouillon
1 × 15 ml spoon/1 tablespoon coarsely chopped parsley	1 tablespoon coarsely chopped parsley
bread sticks	bread sticks

Heat the oil in a saucepan and sauté the garlic until tender. Stir in the rice and continue to sauté until the rice is golden brown, stirring all the time to prevent burning.

Stir in the clams, mussels and stock (bouillon). Bring to the boil, then lower heat. Cover and simmer for 15 minutes or until the rice is tender and liquid absorbed. Fluff up the mixture with a fork and stir in the parsley. Serve immediately with bread sticks.

SERVES 4

RISOTTO SALAMI

METRIC/IMPERIAL	AMERICAN
25 g/1 oz butter	2 tablespoons butter
1 onion, chopped	1 onion, chopped
100 g/4 oz mushrooms, sliced	1 cup sliced mushrooms
1 small red pepper, seeded and diced	1 small red pepper, seeded and diced
1 small green pepper, seeded and diced	1 small green pepper, seeded and diced
200 g/7 oz long grain rice	1 cup long grain rice
450 ml/¾ pint chicken stock	2 cups chicken bouillon
salt	salt
freshly ground black pepper	freshly ground black pepper
113 g/4 oz pack salami, diced	¼ lb salami, diced
113 g/4 oz pack chicken roll, diced	¼ lb chicken roll, diced
100 g/4 oz peeled prawns	⅔ cup shelled shrimp
unpeeled prawns to garnish	unshelled shrimp to garnish

Melt the butter in a frying pan (skillet) and sauté the onion for 5 minutes until soft. Add the mushrooms and peppers and cook for a further 3 minutes. Add the rice, stock (bouillon) and salt and pepper to taste. Bring the mixture to the boil, then lower the heat. Stir, then cover and simmer for 15 minutes.

When most of the liquid has been absorbed, add the salami, chicken and prawns (shrimp) to heat through. Garnish with the unpeeled prawns (unshelled shrimp) and serve immediately.

SERVES 6

ITALIAN SAUSAGE SOUP

METRIC/IMPERIAL	AMERICAN
1 × 15 ml spoon/1 tablespoon oil	1 tablespoon oil
1 onion, chopped	1 onion, chopped
1 clove garlic, crushed	1 clove garlic, crushed
2 carrots, diced	2 carrots, diced
1 celery stick, chopped	1 celery stalk, chopped
900 ml/1½ pints stock	3¾ cups bouillon
1 large potato, diced	1 large potato, diced
¼ cabbage, shredded	¼ cabbage, shredded
50 g/2 oz peas	⅓ cup peas
1 × 396 g/14 oz can tomatoes	1 × 16 oz can tomatoes
2 × 15 ml spoons/2 tablespoons tomato purée	2 tablespoons tomato paste
227 g/8 oz smoked pork sausage, sliced	½ lb smoked pork sausage, sliced
100 g/4 oz rice	½ cup rice
1 × 5 ml spoon/1 teaspoon dried oregano	1 teaspoon dried oregano
salt	salt
freshly ground black pepper	freshly ground black pepper

Heat the oil in a large saucepan, add the onion, garlic, carrots and celery and sauté for 5 minutes until the vegetables are soft. Add the stock (bouillon), remaining vegetables and tomato purée (paste). Cover and cook over a low heat for 40 minutes.

Add the sausage to the soup with the remaining ingredients. Cook for a further 20 minutes. Add salt and pepper to taste. Pour into warm soup bowls and serve immediately.

SERVES 6

STRACCIATELLA

METRIC/IMPERIAL	AMERICAN
600 ml/1 pint consommé or clear chicken soup	2½ cups consommé or clear chicken bouillon
4 eggs	4 eggs
2 × 15 ml spoons/2 tablespoons grated Parmesan cheese	2 tablespoons grated Parmesan cheese
1 × 15 ml spoon/1 tablespoon semolina	1 tablespoon semolina
1 × 15 ml spoon/1 tablespoon chopped parsley	1 tablespoon chopped parsley
salt	salt
freshly ground black pepper	freshly ground black pepper

Pour the soup (bouillon) into a saucepan and heat to boiling. Beat the eggs in a bowl with the cheese, semolina, parsley, salt and pepper to taste and a little of the soup. Then whisk this mixture in a steady stream into the soup in the pan. The finished soup will have a creamy, very lightly scrambled look. Serve immediately.

SERVES 4

RIBOLLITA

METRIC/IMPERIAL	AMERICAN
225 g/8 oz haricot beans, soaked in water overnight	1 cup plus 2 tablespoons navy beans, soaked in water overnight
1.75 litres/3 pints water	7½ cups water
5 × 15 ml spoons/5 tablespoons olive oil	⅓ cup olive oil
1 onion, chopped	1 onion, chopped
1 clove garlic, crushed	1 clove garlic, crushed
1 celery stick, chopped	1 celery stalk, chopped
2 leeks, thinly sliced	2 leeks, thinly sliced
450 g/1 lb green cabbage, finely shredded	1 lb green cabbage, finely shredded
1 sprig each of thyme and rosemary, tied together	1 sprig of thyme and rosemary, tied together
1 × 15 ml spoon/1 tablespoon tomato purée	1 tablespoon tomato paste
salt	salt
freshly ground black pepper	freshly ground black pepper
2 × 15 ml spoons/2 tablespoons chopped parsley	2 tablespoons chopped parsley
croûtons to serve	croûtons to serve

Place the drained beans in a saucepan. Add the water, bring
to the boil, cover and simmer until tender (about 3 hours).
   When the beans are nearly cooked, heat 3 × 15 ml
spoons/3 tablespoons of the oil in a large saucepan. Add
the onion, garlic and celery and sauté for 10 minutes. Add
the leeks, cabbage and herbs and sauté for 3 to 4 minutes.
   Drain the beans and add the cooking liquid to the
vegetables together with the tomato purée (paste) and salt
and pepper to taste. Bring to the boil and simmer for about
30 minutes. Add the beans, with more water as necessary,
and continue simmering until all the vegetables are tender.
   Remove the herbs and adjust the seasoning. Stir in the
remaining oil and parsley. Pour soup into a large warm soup
tureen. Serve immediately, with the croûtons.
SERVES 6 TO 8

ITALIAN CLEAR SOUP

METRIC/IMPERIAL	AMERICAN
4 thin slices white bread	4 thin slices white bread
600 ml/1 pint consommé or clear chicken soup	2½ cups consommé or clear chicken soup
50 g/2 oz butter	¼ cup butter
1 × 15 ml spoon/1 tablespoon tomato purée	1 tablespoon tomato paste
4 eggs	4 eggs
1 × 15 ml spoon/1 tablespoon grated Parmesan cheese	1 tablespoon grated Parmesan cheese
1 × 15 ml spoon/1 tablespoon chopped parsley	1 tablespoon chopped parsley

Remove the crusts from the slices of bread and cut each
slice into 4 squares. Pour the soup into a saucepan and heat
to boiling. Meanwhile, sauté the bread in the butter until
crisp on both sides. Spread each piece of bread with tomato
purée (paste). Pour the soup into 4 warm soup bowls and
quickly break an egg into each. Add the bread squares and
sprinkle over the cheese and parsley. Serve immediately.
SERVES 4

Ribollita

MINESTRONE

METRIC/IMPERIAL	AMERICAN
100 g/4 oz haricot beans, soaked in water overnight	½ cup navy beans, soaked in water overnight
3 × 15 ml spoons/3 tablespoons oil	3 tablespoons oil
2 onions, chopped	2 onions, chopped
2 cloves garlic, crushed	2 cloves garlic, crushed
2–3 bacon rashers	2–3 bacon slices
4 tomatoes, peeled, seeded and chopped	4 tomatoes, skinned, seeded and chopped
1.73 litres/3 pints water	7½ cups water
1 × 5 ml spoon/1 teaspoon chopped fresh marjoram	1 teaspoon chopped fresh marjoram
1 × 2.5 ml spoon/½ teaspoon chopped fresh thyme	½ teapoon chopped fresh thyme
2 carrots, diced	2 carrots, diced
2 potatoes, diced	2 potatoes, diced
1 small turnip, diced	1 small turnip, diced
1–2 celery sticks, finely sliced	1–2 celery stalks, finely sliced
225 g/8 oz cabbage, shredded	½ lb cabbage, shredded
50 g/2 oz small pasta shapes	½ cup small pasta shapes
1 × 15 ml spoon/1 tablespoon chopped parsley	1 tablespoon chopped parsley
salt	salt
freshly ground black pepper	freshly ground black pepper
3 × 15 ml spoons/3 tablespoons grated Parmesan cheese, plus extra to serve	3 tablespoons grated Parmesan cheese, plus extra to serve

Drain the beans. Heat the oil in a large saucepan, add the onions, garlic and bacon and sauté for 5 minutes until soft. Add the tomatoes, beans, water, marjoram and thyme. Cover and simmer for 2 hours.

Add the carrots and cook for about 10 minutes. Add the potatoes and turnip and cook for 10 more minutes. Add the celery, cabbage and pasta and cook for 5 minutes or until the pasta and all the vegetables are tender. Add the parsley and salt and pepper to taste.

Stir in the Parmesan, then pour soup into individual warm soup bowls. Serve immediately, with extra Parmesan cheese.

SERVES 4 TO 6

CABBAGE AND CHEESE SOUP

METRIC/IMPERIAL	AMERICAN
1 Savoy cabbage	1 Savoy cabbage
salt	salt
12 slices bread, toasted	12 slices bread, toasted
100 g/4 oz bacon rashers, fried	¼ lb bacon slices, fried
250 g/9 oz Fontina cheese, sliced	9 oz Fontina cheese, sliced
pinch of ground cinnamon	pinch of ground cinnamon
freshly ground black pepper	freshly ground black pepper
1 litre/1¾ pints meat stock	4¼ cups meat bouillon
25 g/1 oz butter, diced	2 tablespoons butter, diced

Cook the cabbage in boiling salted water for 15 minutes. Drain thoroughly then very carefully separate the leaves.

Line the bottom of an ovenproof dish with 4 slices of the toast. Cover with half the cabbage, bacon and cheese. Repeat these layers once more, then cover with the remaining 4 slices of toast. Add the cinnamon and pepper to taste to the stock (bouillon) then pour into the dish.

Place in a preheated moderate oven (180°C/350°F, Gas Mark 4) and bake for 30 minutes. Remove from the oven, dot with butter, then bake for a further 20 minutes. Serve immediately.

SERVES 4 TO 6

FISH SOUP

METRIC/IMPERIAL	AMERICAN
1.5 kg/3 lb assorted fish (mullet, sea bass, mackerel, sole)	3 lb assorted fish (snapper, sea bass, mackerel, sole)
600 ml/1 pint water	2½ cups water
salt	salt
4 × 15 ml spoons/4 tablespoons olive oil	¼ cup olive oil
2 large onions, thinly sliced	2 large onions, thinly sliced
2 celery sticks, thinly sliced	2 celery stalks, thinly sliced
2 cloves garlic, finely chopped	2 cloves garlic, finely chopped
2 × 15 ml spoons/2 tablespoons chopped parsley	2 tablespoons chopped parsley
150 ml/¼ pint dry white wine	⅔ cup dry white wine
350 g/12 oz tomatoes, seeded and roughly chopped	1½ cups seeded, roughly chopped tomatoes
1 × 5 ml spoon/1 teaspoon tomato purée	1 teaspoon tomato paste
freshly ground black pepper	freshly ground black pepper
100 g/4 oz cooked peeled prawns	⅔ cup cooked shelled shrimp
6 slices French bread, fried in oil until crisp and golden	6 slices French bread, fried in oil until crisp and golden

Clean and fillet the fish, removing the heads and tails. Put the fish heads, tails and trimmings into a saucepan, add the water and salt and bring to the boil. Simmer gently for 30 minutes. Strain and reserve the stock (bouillon).

Heat the oil in a large heavy based saucepan. Add the onions, celery and garlic and sauté for 7 minutes until golden. Add the parsley and wine and allow to bubble for several minutes until the liquid has reduced by about half. Add the tomatoes, tomato purée (paste), fish stock (bouillon) and salt and pepper to taste. Simmer for 15 minutes.

Cut the fish into thick slices, add to the pan and simmer gently for 10 minutes. Add the prawns (shrimp) and simmer for a further 3 to 5 minutes or until all the fish is cooked.

Adjust the seasoning. Place a slice of fried bread in 6 individual soup bowls. Pour over the soup and serve immediately.

SERVES 6

MUSSEL SOUP

METRIC/IMPERIAL	AMERICAN
2.75 litres/5 pints mussels	12 cups mussels
3 × 15 ml spoons/3 tablespoons olive oil	3 tablespoons olive oil
1 onion, finely chopped	1 onion, finely chopped
1 celery stick, chopped	1 celery stalk, chopped
1 clove garlic, thinly sliced	1 clove garlic, thinly sliced
1 kg/2 lb tomatoes, peeled and chopped	4 cups skinned, chopped tomatoes
1 × 5 ml spoon/1 teaspoon dried oregano	1 teaspoon dried oregano
200 ml/⅓ pint white wine	⅞ cup white wine
200 ml/⅓ pint hot water	⅞ cup hot water

First, prepare the mussels; cover with cold water, discarding any which are open or float to the top. Scrub the mussels to remove any barnacles, and remove the beards. Soak in fresh cold water while you make the soup.

Heat the oil in a large saucepan and sauté the onion for 5 minutes until soft. Add the celery and garlic and sauté for 3 minutes. Add the tomatoes and oregano and cook, stirring, for 5 minutes. Pour over the white wine, cover and cook until the tomatoes are almost reduced to a pulp. Add the hot water and bring the soup to the boil.

Drain the mussels and add to the soup. Boil for 10 to 12 minutes, stirring occasionally, until all the mussels have opened. Discard any mussels that do not open. Serve immediately. Place extra plates on the table for the discarded shells.

SERVES 4

Fish Soup

COURGETTE (ZUCCHINI) SOUP

METRIC/IMPERIAL	AMERICAN
50 g/2 oz butter	¼ cup butter
1 medium onion, sliced	1 medium onion, sliced
750 g/1½ lb courgettes, sliced	1½ lb zucchini, sliced
1.75 litres/3 pints water	7½ cups water
2 chicken stock cubes	2 chicken bouillon cubes
2 eggs	2 eggs
3 × 15 ml spoons/3 tablespoons grated Parmesan cheese	3 tablespoons grated Parmesan cheese
2 × 15 ml spoons/2 tablespoons chopped fresh basil or parsley	2 tablespoons chopped fresh basil or parsley
salt	salt
freshly ground black pepper	freshly ground black pepper
grated Parmesan cheese to serve	grated Parmesan cheese to serve

Melt the butter in a large saucepan and sauté the onion for 5 minutes until soft. Add the courgettes (zucchini) and sauté for 5 to 10 minutes until lightly golden. Add the water, crumble in the stock (bouillon) cubes, bring to the boil, cover and simmer gently for about 20 minutes.

Purée the mixture in an electric blender, then return to the saucepan. Bring the soup to the boil. Put the eggs, cheese, herbs and salt and pepper in the bottom of a large warm soup tureen, and, using a whisk, beat together thoroughly. Still whisking, pour the boiling soup slowly onto the beaten eggs. Serve immediately with extra Parmesan cheese.

SERVES 6 TO 8

PASTA

SPAGHETTI CARBONARA

METRIC/IMPERIAL	AMERICAN
350 g/12 oz spaghetti	¾ lb spaghetti
salt	salt
175 g/6 oz streaky bacon rashers, cut into 1 cm/½ inch strips	9 fatty bacon slices, cut into ½ inch strips
3 eggs	3 eggs
2 × 15 ml spoons/2 tablespoons single cream	2 tablespoons light cream
40 g/1½ oz grated Parmesan or Pecorino cheese	6 tablespoons grated Parmesan or Pecorino cheese
freshly ground black pepper	freshly ground black pepper
40 g/1½ oz butter	3 tablespoons butter

Cook the spaghetti in a large pan of boiling salted water for about 10 minutes or until tender but *al dente*. Drain thoroughly.

Sauté the bacon gently in a frying pan (skillet) until crisp and golden. Beat the eggs with the cream and cheese and season with salt and pepper.

Heat the butter in a large saucepan, add the egg mixture and stir over a moderate heat until just beginning to thicken. Quickly add the fried bacon and the spaghetti and toss lightly together. Serve immediately.
SERVES 4

SPAGHETTI MOZZARELLA

METRIC/IMPERIAL	AMERICAN
350 g/12 oz spaghetti	¾ lb spaghetti
salt	salt
100 g/4 oz butter	½ cup butter
1 clove garlic, crushed	1 clove garlic, crushed
2 × 15 ml spoons/2 tablespoons olive oil	2 tablespoons olive oil
4 tomatoes, cut into sections	4 tomatoes, cut into sections
75 g/3 oz black olives	½ cup ripe olives
175 g/6 oz Mozzarella or Bel Paese cheese, cubed	1 cup cubed Mozzarella or Bel Paese cheese
3 × 15 ml spoons/3 tablespoons chopped parsley	3 tablespoons chopped parsley
freshly ground black pepper	freshly ground black pepper

Cook the spaghetti in a large pan of boiling salted water for about 10 minutes until tender but *al dente*.

Meanwhile put the butter in a small saucepan and stir over a gentle heat until it turns a nutty brown colour. Stir in the garlic and olive oil.

Drain the spaghetti thoroughly and toss in the hot butter, together with the tomatoes, olives, cubed cheese, parsley and salt and pepper to taste. Serve immediately.
SERVES 4

SPAGHETTI MARINARA

METRIC/IMPERIAL	AMERICAN
225 g/8 oz spaghetti	½ lb spaghetti
salt	salt
25 g/1 oz butter	2 tablespoons butter
25 g/1 oz plain flour	¼ cup all-purpose flour
300 ml/½ pint milk	1¼ cups milk
1 × 5 ml spoon/1 teaspoon tomato purée	1 teaspoon tomato paste
freshly ground black pepper	freshly ground black pepper
100 g/4 oz cooked peas	¾ cup cooked peas
50 g/2 oz cooked sweetcorn	⅓ cup cooked whole kernel corn
450 g/1 lb cooked and flaked white fish (cod, whiting)	1 lb cooked and flaked white fish (cod, whiting)

Cook the spaghetti in a large pan of boiling salted water for about 10 minutes until tender but *al dente*.

Meanwhile place the butter and flour in a small saucepan over a moderate heat and blend until smooth; add milk gradually and bring to the boil, whisking continuously until smooth. Stir in the remaining ingredients. Drain the spaghetti thoroughly and arrange in individual warm dishes. Pour over the sauce and serve immediately.
SERVES 4

EGG 'N' SPAGHETTI

METRIC/IMPERIAL	AMERICAN
225 g/8 oz spaghetti	½ lb spaghetti
salt	salt
100 g/4 oz streaky bacon rashers, cooked and diced	¼ lb fatty bacon slices, cooked and diced
50 g/2 oz mushrooms, sliced	½ cup sliced mushrooms
1 × 5 ml spoon/1 teaspoon dried oregano	1 teaspoon dried oregano
4 eggs, beaten	4 eggs, beaten
50 g/2 oz Cheddar cheese, grated	½ cup grated Cheddar cheese
freshly ground black pepper	freshly ground black pepper

Cook the spaghetti in a large pan of boiling salted water for about 10 minutes until tender but *al dente*. Drain thoroughly and return to the pan.

Add the bacon, mushrooms, oregano and eggs. Cook until the eggs are just beginning to set. Add the cheese and cook for a few more minutes. Season with salt and pepper. Place in a warm serving dish and serve immediately.
SERVES 4

Spaghetti Carbonara

EGG PASTA VERDE

METRIC/IMPERIAL	AMERICAN
225 g/8 oz plain flour	2 cups all-purpose flour
salt	salt
2 eggs	2 eggs
50 g/2 oz finely chopped cooked spinach	1/4 cup finely chopped cooked spinach
2 × 5 ml spoons/2 teaspoons oil	2 teaspoons oil
few drops of water (as necessary)	few drops of water (as necessary)

Sieve the flour and salt onto a board. Make a well in the centre and add the eggs, spinach and oil. Carefully work flour into liquid, adding a few drops of water where the mixture seems dry.

Flour the board and your hands then knead pasta until smooth. Wrap the dough in plastic wrap and set aside for about 1 hour.

Roll out the dough on a floured surface until it is paper thin. Dust the pasta lightly with flour and leave to rest for 10 to 20 minutes, so that it dries a little and becomes less inclined to stick. Use to make flat pasta shapes (tagliatelle, fettuccine, lasagne). Cook pasta in a large pan of boiling salted water for 5 minutes until tender but *al dente*.

MAKES ABOUT 350 g/12 oz (¾ lb) pasta

TAGLIATELLE BOLOGNESE

METRIC/IMPERIAL	AMERICAN
450 g/1 lb tagliatelle	1 lb tagliatelle
40 g/1½ oz butter, melted	3 tablespoons butter, melted
2–3 × 15 ml spoons/2–3 tablespoons grated Parmesan cheese, plus extra to serve	2–3 tablespoons grated Parmesan cheese, plus extra to serve
Sauce:	Sauce:
15 g/½ oz butter	1 tablespoon butter
1 onion, finely chopped	1 onion, finely chopped
1 small carrot, finely chopped	1 small carrot, finely chopped
1 celery stick, finely chopped	1 celery stalk, finely chopped
3 streaky bacon rashers, finely chopped	3 fatty bacon slices, finely chopped
350 g/12 oz finely minced beef	1½ cups finely ground beef
100 g/4 oz chicken livers, finely chopped	1/4 lb chicken livers, finely chopped
4 × 15 ml spoons/4 tablespoons dry white wine or dry vermouth	1/4 cup dry white wine or dry vermouth
300 ml/½ pint beef stock	1¼ cups beef bouillon
1 × 15 ml spoon/1 tablespoon tomato purée	1 tablespoon tomato paste
grated nutmeg	grated nutmeg
salt	salt
freshly ground black pepper	freshly ground black pepper
3 × 15 ml spoons/3 tablespoons double cream	3 tablespoons heavy cream

First, make the sauce: melt the butter in a large frying pan (skillet). Add the onion, carrot, celery and bacon and sauté for about 10 minutes until golden brown. Add the beef and sauté, stirring, for 5 minutes, until browned.

Add the chicken livers and cook, stirring, for 2 minutes, then add the wine and simmer until it has almost completely evaporated. Stir in the stock (bouillon), tomato purée (paste), nutmeg, salt and pepper to taste. Bring to the boil, cover and simmer very gently for 1 hour, stirring occasionally. Stir in the cream.

Cook the tagliatelle in a large pan of boiling salted water for about 10 minutes until tender but *al dente*. Drain the tagliatelle thoroughly.

Pour the melted butter into a warm deep serving dish and add the drained tagliatelle. Add about 4 × 15 ml spoons/4 tablespoons of the hot sauce and a little of the cheese, and toss lightly with 2 forks until the pasta is well coated. Pile the remaining sauce on top. Serve immediately with extra Parmesan cheese.

SERVES 4 TO 6

VERMICELLI WITH TOMATO AND MUSSEL SAUCE

METRIC/IMPERIAL	AMERICAN
2.25 litres/4 pints fresh mussels	10 cups fresh mussels
150 ml/¼ pint water	⅔ cup water
5 × 15 ml spoons/5 tablespoons olive oil	⅓ cup olive oil
1 medium onion, finely chopped	1 medium onion, finely chopped
2 cloves garlic, sliced	2 cloves garlic, sliced
750 g/1½ lb tomatoes, peeled and chopped	3 cups skinned, chopped tomatoes
350 g/12 oz vermicelli or spaghetti	¾ ml vermicelli or spaghetti
salt	salt
freshly ground black pepper	freshly ground black pepper
2 × 15 ml spoons/2 tablespoons chopped parsley to garnish	2 tablespoons chopped parsley to garnish

First, prepare the mussels: cover with cold water, discarding any which are open or float to the top. Scrub the mussels to remove any barnacles and remove beards. Soak in fresh cold water until ready to cook.

Put mussels into a large pan with the water and heat briskly, shaking the pan occasionally, for 5 to 6 minutes or until the shells open. Discard any mussels that do not open. Remove from the heat and drain off the water. Set aside a few of the mussels in their shells to garnish. Discard the shells from the rest of the mussels.

Heat 3 × 15 ml spoons/3 tablespoons of the oil in a large saucepan. Add the onion and sauté for 5 minutes until soft. Stir in the garlic, then the tomatoes. Simmer gently for about 30 minutes until the tomatoes have reduced to a pulp.

Cook the pasta in a large pan of boiling salted water for about 10 minutes until tender but al dente. Drain thoroughly. Pour the remaining oil into a warm dish, add the pasta and toss until lightly coated.

Season the sauce with salt and pepper, add the shelled mussels and heat through, stirring. Pile the sauce on top of the pasta. Garnish with the reserved mussels and chopped parsley and serve immediately.

SERVES 4

Vermicelli with Tomato and Mussel Sauce

TAGLIATELLE WITH TUNA

METRIC/IMPERIAL	AMERICAN
350 g/12 oz tagliatelle	¾ lb tagliatelle
salt	salt
1 × 198 g/7 oz can tuna fish in oil, drained and flaked with oil reserved	1 × 7 oz can tuna fish in oil, drained and flaked with oil reserved
1 medium onion, finely chopped	1 medium onion, finely chopped
100 g/4 oz mushrooms, sliced	1 cup sliced mushrooms
freshly ground black pepper	freshly ground black pepper
150 ml/¼ pint double cream	⅔ cup heavy cream

Pour the oil from the tuna fish into a saucepan. Sauté the onion in the oil over moderate heat for 5 minutes until soft, then add the mushrooms and cook for a further 5 minutes. Add salt and pepper to taste.

Meanwhile cook the tagliatelle in a large pan of boiling salted water until tender, drain thoroughly and return to the pan. Add the tuna, onion and mushrooms. Pour in the cream and mix all the ingredients together. Cook over low heat to warm cream. Adjust seasoning and serve immediately.

SERVES 4

LASAGNE AL FORNO

METRIC/IMPERIAL	AMERICAN
225 g/8 oz pre-cooked green or plain lasagne	½ lb pre-cooked green or plain lasagne
salt	salt
Meat sauce	Meat sauce:
15 g/½ oz butter	1 tablespoon butter
1 onion, finely chopped	1 onion, finely chopped
1 small carrot, finely chopped	1 small carrot, finely chopped
1 celery stick, finely chopped	1 celery stalk, finely chopped
3 streaky bacon rashers, finely chopped	3 fatty bacon slices, finely chopped
350 g/12 oz finely minced beef	1½ cups finely ground beef
100 g/4 oz chicken livers, finely chopped	¼ lb chicken livers, finely chopped
4 × 15 ml spoons/4 tablespoons red wine	¼ cup red wine
300 ml/½ pint beef stock	1¼ cups beef bouillon
1 × 15 ml spoon/1 tablespoon tomato purée	1 tablespoon tomato paste
grated nutmeg	grated nutmeg
salt	salt
freshly ground black pepper	freshly ground black pepper
White sauce:	White sauce:
40 g/1½ oz butter	3 tablespoons butter
40 g/1½ oz flour	6 tablespoons flour
600 ml/1 pint hot milk	2½ cups hot milk
4 × 15 ml spoons/4 tablespoons double cream	¼ cup heavy cream
grated nutmeg	grated nutmeg
50 g/2 oz grated Parmesan cheese	½ cup grated Parmesan cheese

First, make the meat sauce: melt the bu[..] a large frying pan (skillet). Add the onion, carrot, cel[..] and bacon and sauté for about 10 minutes until golden brown. Add the beef and sauté, stirring, for 5 minutes, until browned.

Add the chicken livers and cook, stirring, for 2 minutes, then add the wine and simmer until it has almost completely evaporated. Stir in the stock (bouillon), tomato purée (paste), nutmeg, salt and pepper to taste. Bring to the boil, cover and simmer very gently for 1 hour, stirring occasionally.

To make the white sauce: melt the butter in a saucepan, stir in the flour and cook for 1 minute. Remove from the heat and pour in the milk and cream, beating continuously with a wire whisk. Return to a high heat and stir until thick and smooth. Simmer over a low heat for 2 to 3 minutes. Season with salt and nutmeg.

Butter a large shallow ovenproof serving dish. Spread a layer of meat sauce over the bottom, cover with an overlapping layer of lasagne, then a layer of white sauce and a sprinkling of Parmesan cheese. Repeat the layers, finishing with a thick layer of white sauce and cheese.

Place in a preheated moderate oven (180°C/350°F, Gas Mark 4) and bake for about 30 minutes until golden brown on top. Serve immediately.

SERVES 6 TO 8

RAVIOLI

METRIC/IMPERIAL	AMERICAN
Pasta:	Pasta:
750 g/1½ lb plain flour	6 cups all-p[..]ose flour
salt	salt
2 large eggs, beaten	2 large eggs, beaten
2 × 15 ml spoons/2 tablespoons olive oil	2 tablespoons olive oil
175 ml/6 fl oz water	¾ cup water
Filling:	Filling:
225 g/8 oz Ricotta or cottage cheese	1 cup Ricotta or cottage cheese
350 g/12 oz cooked minced beef	1½ cups cooked ground beef
1 egg	1 egg
1 × 15 ml spoon/1 tablespoon chopped parsley	1 tablespoon chopped parsley
salt	salt
freshly ground black pepper	freshly ground black pepper
grated Parmesan cheese to serve	grated Parmesan cheese to serve

To make the pasta: sieve the flour and salt onto a board. Make a well in the centre and add the eggs, olive oil and water. Carefully work flour into liquid. Flour the board and your hands then knead pasta until smooth. Cut pasta in half. Roll out each half thinly into a strip, 3 × 45 cm/ 12 × 18 inches. Cut in half lengthwise.

To make the filling: mix together Ricotta or cottage cheese, cold beef, egg, parsley and salt and pepper to taste. Place 48 small teaspoons of the mixture over one pasta strip, making 8 rows with 6 mounds of filling in each row. Dampen edges of pasta, then lay the other pasta strip over the top, sealing the edges well. Cut out ravioli using a pastry cutter and seal edges well. Chill. Repeat with other piece of pasta.

Drop ravioli into gently boiling water and cook for 10 to 15 minutes. Drain well. Serve immediately with Parmesan cheese.

SERVES 12 as a starter, or 8 as a main course

TORTELLINI

METRIC/IMPERIAL	AMERICAN
40 g/1½ oz butter	3 tablespoons butter
175 g/6 oz raw turkey breast meat, sliced	6 oz raw turkey breast meat, sliced
75 g/3 oz cooked ham	3 oz processed ham
75 g/3 oz Mortadella sausage	3 oz Mortadella sausage
4 × 15 ml spoons/4 tablespoons grated Parmesan cheese	¼ cup grated Parmesan cheese
2 eggs, beaten	2 eggs, beaten
salt	salt
freshly ground black pepper	freshly ground black pepper
350 g/12 oz egg pasta	¾ lb egg pasta
To serve:	To serve:
1.2 litres/2 pints chicken broth	5 cups chicken bouillon
1–2 chicken stock cubes (optional)	1–2 chicken bouillon cubes (optional)
grated Parmesan cheese to serve	grated Parmesan cheese to serve

Melt the butter in a frying pan (skillet) and sauté the turkey slices gently for about 12 minutes until golden. Pass the fried turkey, ham and Mortadella through the fine blades of a mincer, twice. Add the cheese and eggs with salt and pepper to taste and mix thoroughly to form a smooth paste. Place in a bowl, cover and refrigerate.

Prepare the pasta (see above) and roll out very thinly to a large square. Dust lightly with flour and leave to rest and dry for 15 to 20 minutes. Cut into approximately forty 4 cm/1½ inch squares and place about 1 × 2.5 ml spoon/½ teaspoon of filling on each square. Dampen edges and fold each square to form a triangle, enclosing the filling. Press the edges together firmly to seal. Curve each triangle around your fingertip and press the two ends together.

Bring the broth (bouillon) to the boil, adding the stock (bouillon) cubes if necessary. Drop in the tortellini and simmer, stirring occasionally, for 5 minutes. Turn off the heat, cover the pan and leave to stand for 25 minutes. Ladle the tortellini into warm soup plates with a little of the broth. Serve immediately with grated Parmesan.

SERVES 4

CANNELLONI

METRIC/IMPERIAL	AMERICAN
8 pieces wide lasagne	8 pieces wide lasagne
1 × 15 ml spoon/1 tablespoon vegetable oil	1 tablespoon vegetable oil
Filling:	Filling:
2 × 15 ml spoons/2 tablespoons olive oil	2 tablespoons olive oil
50 g/2 oz onion, finely chopped	½ cup finely chopped onion
1 clove garlic, crushed	1 clove garlic, crushed
225 g/8 oz lean beef, finely minced	1 cup finely ground beef
2 tomatoes, peeled, seeded and chopped	2 tomatoes, skinned, seeded and chopped
1 × 15 ml spoon/1 tablespoon fine breadcrumbs	1 tablespoon fine bread crumbs
25 g/1 oz grated Parmesan cheese	¼ cup grated Parmesan cheese
1 × 5 ml spoon/1 teaspoon chopped fresh marjoram or ½ × 2.5 ml spoon/¼ teaspoon dried marjoram	1 teaspoon chopped fresh marjoram or ¼ teaspoon dried marjoram
1 egg, lightly beaten	1 egg, lightly beaten
salt	salt
freshly ground black pepper	freshly ground black pepper
Sauce:	Sauce:
40 g/1½ oz butter	3 tablespoons butter
40 g/1½ oz flour	⅓ cup flour
300 ml/½ pint hot milk	1¼ cups hot milk
150 ml/¼ pint hot single cream	⅔ cup hot light cream
salt	salt
white pepper	white pepper
grated nutmeg	grated nutmeg
Topping:	Topping:
25 g/1 oz grated Parmesan cheese	¼ cup grated Parmesan cheese
15 g/½ oz butter	1 tablespoon butter

To prepare the filling: heat the oil in a saucepan, add the onion and garlic and sauté for 5 minutes until soft. Add the minced (ground) meat and cook, stirring, until the meat browns. Add the tomatoes, cover and cook gently for 10 minutes. Remove the pan from the heat and stir in the breadcrumbs, cheese, marjoram, egg, salt and pepper. Leave to cool.

To make the sauce: melt the butter in a saucepan, remove from the heat and add the flour, then cook very gently for about a minute, stirring all the time. Remove from the heat, add the milk and cream all at once and beat with a wire whisk until smooth. Return to the heat and bring to the boil, whisking all the time. Season the sauce to taste with salt, pepper and nutmeg. Cover with greaseproof (waxed) paper and a lid and keep warm.

To cook the pasta: cook lasagne with the oil in a large pan of boiling salted water, a few pieces at a time, for about 10 minutes until tender, but *al dente*. Remove lasagne with a slotted spoon, drain well, lay flat side by side on a clean cloth, and leave to cool a little.

Spoon a little of the filling down one long side of each piece of pasta and roll each one up into a cylinder. Arrange the cylinders side by side in a well buttered ovenproof dish. Spoon the sauce over the pasta, making sure it is completely covered. Sprinkle with Parmesan cheese and dot with butter.

Place the dish, uncovered, in a preheated moderately hot oven (190°C/375°F, Gas Mark 5) and bake for 20 to 30 minutes until bubbling hot and golden. Remove and serve immediately.

SERVES 4

SPINACH GNOCCHI

METRIC/IMPERIAL	AMERICAN
450 g/1 lb fresh spinach, or 1 × 400 g/14 oz packet frozen spinach	1 lb fresh spinach or 1 × 14 oz packet frozen spinach
100 g/4 oz Ricotta or cottage cheese	½ cup Ricotta or cottage cheese
salt	salt
freshly ground black pepper	freshly ground black pepper
1 × 5 ml spoon/1 teaspoon grated nutmeg	1 teaspoon grated nutmeg
15 g/½ oz butter	1 tablespoon butter
25 g/1 oz grated Parmesan cheese	¼ cup grated Parmesan cheese
1 egg	1 egg
40 g/1½ oz plain flour	6 tablespoons all-purpose flour
To serve:	To serve:
25–50 g/1–2 oz butter, melted	2–4 tablespoons melted butter
25–50 g/1–2 oz grated Parmesan cheese for topping	¼–½ cup grated Parmesan cheese for topping

Wash fresh spinach and cook with the water that clings to the leaves in a covered pan for 3 minutes. Cook frozen spinach according to packet directions.

Drain, squeeze and finely chop spinach. Sieve the Ricotta or cottage cheese. Return the spinach to the pan with salt, pepper, nutmeg and butter. Add the Ricotta or cottage cheese. Stir over low heat for 5 minutes. Remove from the heat and beat in the 25 g/1 oz (¼ cup) grated Parmesan cheese, egg and flour. Turn onto a plate and flatten. Leave to cool for several hours.

Using a little flour, shape the mixture into small croquettes. Drop the spinach gnocchi into a large pan of boiling salted water and cook for about 5 minutes. When they are cooked they will rise to the top. Drain the gnocchi in a colander. Toss carefully in melted butter. Lightly grease an ovenproof dish and dredge with Parmesan cheese. Arrange gnocchi in dish and dredge with more Parmesan. Place in a preheated moderate oven (180°C/350°F, Gas Mark 4) and cook for 5 minutes. Serve immediately.

SERVES 4

Gnocchi with Pesto

GNOCCHI WITH PESTO

METRIC/IMPERIAL	AMERICAN
450 g/1 lb potatoes, freshly boiled	1 lb potatoes, freshly boiled
175 g/6 oz plain flour	1½ cups all-purpose flour
1 egg, beaten	1 egg, beaten
salt	salt
freshly ground black pepper	freshly ground black pepper
grated nutmeg	grated nutmeg
Pesto:	Pesto:
50 g/2 oz fresh basil leaves	2 oz fresh basil leaves
25 g/1 oz pine nuts or walnuts	¼ cup pine nuts or walnuts
2 cloves garlic	2 cloves garlic
salt	salt
freshly ground black pepper	freshly ground black pepper
4 × 15 ml spoons/4 tablespoons olive oil	¼ cup olive oil
40 g/1½ oz grated Parmesan or Pecorino cheese	⅓ cup grated Parmesan or Pecorino cheese
To serve:	To serve:
25 g/1 oz butter	2 tablespoons butter
grated Parmesan cheese	grated Parmesan cheese

First, make the pesto: chop the basil and nuts roughly and put into a mortar with the garlic, salt and pepper. Pound together until reduced to a thick paste. Add the oil a little at a time, stirring constantly as for a mayonnaise, until the sauce is the consistency of thick cream. Alternatively, purée in an electric blender. Stir in the cheese. Cover the sauce and set aside.

Make the gnocchi: drain the potatoes well and shake over the heat to dry thoroughly. Mash very finely (there should be no lumps) and add the flour, egg and salt, pepper and nutmeg to taste. Mix to a dough and turn onto a floured board.

With floured hands, roll pieces of the dough into small croquettes. Using your little finger, make a dent in the centre of each one to make them curl slightly.

Drop the gnocchi, a few at a time, into a large pan of boiling salted water and cook for about 3 to 5 minutes. When they are cooked they will rise to the top. Lift out with a slotted spoon and drain. Lightly grease a serving dish. Arrange gnocchi in the dish and keep hot. Cook remaining gnocchi.

Dot with butter and sprinkle with cheese. Thin the pesto down with a little of the gnocchi cooking water. Pour pesto over gnocchi and serve immediately.
SERVES 4

PIZZAS AND QUICK SNACKS

NEAPOLITAN-STYLE PIZZA

METRIC/IMPERIAL	AMERICAN
Base:	Base:
15 g/½ oz fresh yeast	½ cake compressed yeast
2 × 15 ml spoons/2 tablespoons warm water	2 tablespoons warm water
225 g/8 oz plain flour	2 cups all-purpose flour
salt	salt
2 × 15 ml spoons/2 tablespoons olive oil	2 tablespoons olive oil
3 × 15 ml spoons/3 tablespoons milk	3 tablespoons milk
Topping:	Topping:
4 × 15 ml spoons/4 tablespoons olive oil	¼ cup olive oil
1 × 400 g/14 oz can peeled tomatoes, drained	1 × 14 oz can peeled tomatoes, drained
salt	salt
freshly ground black pepper	freshly ground black pepper
1 × 15 ml spoon/1 tablespoon chopped fresh basil	1 tablespoons chopped fresh basil
1 × 5 ml spoon/1 teaspoon dried oregano	1 teaspoon dried oregano
175 g/6 oz Mozzarella or Bel Paese cheese, sliced	6 oz Mozzarella or Bel Paese cheese, sliced
4 × 15 ml spoons/4 tablespoons grated Parmesan cheese	¼ cup grated Parmesan cheese

Blend the yeast with the water. Leave in a warm place for 10 minutes until frothy. Sieve the flour and salt onto a board, make a well in the centre and pour in the yeast mixture, oil and milk. With one hand, gradually draw the flour into the liquids and mix to form a stiff but pliable dough, adding more milk if necessary. Knead the dough for 5 minutes. Gather into a ball, place in an oiled polythene bag and leave in a warm place for 1 hour until doubled in size.

Turn the dough onto a floured surface and divide into 2 or 4 pieces, depending on the size of pizzas required. Knead each piece lightly and place on well oiled aluminium pie plates, either two 23 cm/9 inch plates or four 15 cm/6 inch plates. With floured knuckles, press out the dough to cover the base of the plates and reach 1 cm/½ inch up the side.

Brush with oil, cover with the chopped tomatoes and season with salt and pepper. Sprinkle with basil and oregano. Place the cheese on top and sprinkle with Parmesan. (Anchovy fillets, black olives, sliced mushrooms or sausage can also be added to the topping.) Sprinkle oil over each pizza. Leave to rise in a warm place for 30 minutes.

Place in a preheated hot oven (220°C/425°F, Gas Mark 7) and bake for 15 minutes. Reduce the heat to moderate (180°C/350°F, Gas Mark 4) and bake for another 5 to 10 minutes. Serve immediately.

SERVES 4 TO 8

TOMATO, OLIVE AND SALAMI PIZZA

METRIC/IMPERIAL	AMERICAN
Scone base:	Biscuit base:
225 g/8 oz self-raising flour	2 cups self-rising flour
1 × 5 ml spoon/1 teaspoon baking powder	1 teaspoon baking powder
salt	salt
25 g/1 oz softened butter	2 tablespoons softened butter
150 ml/¼ pint milk	⅔ cup milk
2 × 15 ml spoons/2 tablespoons French mustard	2 tablespoons French-style mustard
Topping:	Topping:
1 × 800 g/1 lb 12 oz can tomatoes	1 × 1 lb 12 oz can tomatoes
1 onion, chopped	1 onion, chopped
2 × 15 ml spoons/2 tablespoons tomato purée	2 tablespoons tomato paste
2 × 5 ml spoons/2 teaspoons dried oregano	2 teaspoons dried oregano
1 × 5 ml spoon/1 teaspoon sugar	1 teaspoon sugar
salt	salt
freshly ground black pepper	freshly ground black pepper
175 g/6 oz Mozzarella cheese, sliced	6 oz Mozzarella cheese, sliced
100 g/4 oz salami, sliced	¼ lb salami, sliced
50 g/2 oz stuffed green olives, halved	½ cup stuffed green olives, halved
1 × 15 ml spoon/1 tablespoon grated Parmesan cheese	1 tablespoon grated Parmesan cheese

First, make the topping: put the tomatoes with their juice, onion, tomato purée (paste), oregano and sugar into a pan and season with salt and pepper. Cook gently for about 30 minutes, uncovered, to reduce the mixture to a thick pulp. Adjust seasoning to taste.

Meanwhile, make the scone (biscuit) base: sieve the flour, baking powder and salt into a large bowl. Rub (cut) in the butter and mix to a soft dough with the milk. Turn onto a large floured baking sheet, then roll out to a 25 cm/ 10 inch round. Spread mustard over the pizza base.

Spread the tomato mixture over the dough to within 2.5 cm/1 inch of the edge. Arrange Mozzarella, salami and olives on the tomato mixture, and sprinkle with Parmesan cheese.

Place in a preheated moderately hot oven (200°C/400°F, Gas Mark 6) and bake for about 30 to 40 minutes until well risen and golden brown. Serve immediately.

SERVES 6 TO 8

Neapolitan-style Pizza

PAN PIZZA

METRIC/IMPERIAL

Base:
100 g/4 oz plain flour
salt
1 × 5 ml spoon/1 teaspoon
   baking powder
4 × 15 ml spoons/4
   tablespoons water
3 × 15 ml spoons/3
   tablespoons oil
Topping:
1 × 113 g/4 oz packet liver
   pâté
1 × 227 g/8 oz can tomatoes,
   drained and chopped
50 g/2 oz beer sausage, cut
   into strips
50 g/2 oz haslet, cut into strips
50 g/2 oz Cheddar cheese,
   grated
25 g/1 oz grated Parmesan
   cheese
1 × 15 ml spoon/1 tablespoon
   chopped parsley

AMERICAN

Base:
1 cup all-purpose flour
salt
1 teaspoon baking powder
4 tablespoons water
3 tablespoons oil
Topping:
¼ lb packet liver pâté
1 × 8 oz can tomatoes,
   drained and chopped
2 oz beer sausage, cut into
   strips
2 oz haslet, cut into strips
½ cup grated Cheddar cheese
¼ cup grated Parmesan
   cheese
1 tablespoon chopped parsley

Sieve the flour, salt and baking powder into a bowl. Make a well in the centre and add sufficient water to make a fairly firm dough. Knead for a few minutes, then roll out on a lightly floured surface into a thin round about 18 cm/7 inch in diameter.

Heat the oil in a heavy frying pan (skillet) and add the pizza base. Cook for 5 minutes or until the underside is golden brown. Turn the base over. Spread the pâté over the base and cover with the tomatoes. Arrange meat strips on the tomatoes and cover with the cheeses. Cover the pan and cook for about 10 minutes, or until the cheese is melted. Place under a preheated hot grill (broiler) for 3 minutes to brown. Sprinkle over the parsley and serve immediately.

SERVES 2 TO 3

TOMATO AND SALAMI PIZZA

METRIC/IMPERIAL	AMERICAN
Scone base:	Biscuit base:
225 g/8 oz self-raising flour	2 cups self-rising flour
1 × 5 ml spoon/1 teaspoon baking powder	1 teaspoon baking powder
1 × 2.5 ml spoon/½ teaspoon dry mustard	½ teaspoon dry mustard
salt	salt
50 g/2 oz soft margarine	¼ cup soft margarine
1 × 2.5 ml spoon/½ teaspoon dried mixed herbs	½ teaspoon dried mixed herbs
7 × 15 ml spoons/7 tablespoons milk	7 tablespoons milk
Topping:	Topping:
100 g/4 oz grated cheese	1 cup grated cheese
100 g/4 oz salami, sliced	¼ lb salami, sliced
2 tomatoes, sliced	2 tomatoes, sliced
1 × 2.5 ml spoon/½ teaspoon dried oregano	½ teaspoon dried oregano
2 slices ham, cut into strips	2 slices ham, cut into strips
parsley sprigs to garnish	parsley sprigs to garnish

Sieve the flour, baking powder, mustard and salt into a bowl. Rub (cut) in the margarine and add the herbs. Mix to a soft dough with the milk. Knead lightly and roll out on a lightly floured surface to a 23 cm/9 inch round. Place on a greased baking sheet.

Sprinkle with the cheese and arrange salami and tomatoes on top. Sprinkle over oregano and arrange a lattice of ham strips on top. Place in a moderately hot oven (200°C/400°F, Gas Mark 6) and bake for 20 to 25 minutes. Garnish with parsley sprigs and serve immediately.
SERVES 4 TO 6

TUNA PIZZA

METRIC/IMPERIAL	AMERICAN
Base:	Base:
1 × 5 ml spoon/1 teaspoon paprika	1 teaspoon paprika
1 × 275 g/10 oz packet white bread mix	1 × 10 oz packet white bread mix
2 × 15 ml spoons/2 tablespoons tomato purée	2 tablespoons tomato paste
200 ml/⅓ pint hot water	1 cup hot water
Topping:	Topping:
1 × 15 ml spoon/1 tablespoon olive oil	1 tablespoon olive oil
1 large onion, sliced	1 large onion, sliced
1 × 198 g/7 oz can tuna, drained and flaked	1 × 7 oz can tuna, drained and flaked
175 g/6 oz Cheddar cheese, grated	1½ cups grated Cheddar cheese
salt	salt
freshly ground black pepper	freshly ground black pepper

Add the paprika to the bread mix. Blend the tomato purée (paste) in the hot water and add it to the bread mix. Follow packet directions up to the point for kneading for 5 minutes. Roll out the dough on a lightly floured surface to a 30 cm/12 inch round and place on a greased baking sheet.

Heat the olive oil in a small frying pan (skillet) and sauté the onion for 5 minutes until soft. Spread the onion over the base. Cover with flaked tuna and grated cheese. Add salt and pepper to taste. Place in a preheated hot oven (220°C/425°F, Gas Mark 7) and bake for 20 minutes. Serve immediately.
SERVES 4

WHOLEWHEAT PIZZA

METRIC/IMPERIAL	AMERICAN
Base:	Base:
15 g/½ oz fresh yeast or 1½ × 5 ml spoons/1½ teaspoons dried yeast and 1 × 2.5 ml spoon/½ teaspoon sugar	½ cake compressed yeast or 1½ teaspoons dried yeast and ½ teaspoon sugar
6–7 × 15 ml spoons/6–7 tablespoons warm milk	6–7 tablespoons warm milk
225 g/8 oz wholewheat flour	1 cup wholewheat flour
salt	salt
freshly ground black pepper	freshly ground black pepper
25 g/1 oz butter	2 tablespoons butter
Topping:	Topping:
1 × 15 ml spoon/1 tablespoon olive oil	1 tablespoon olive oil
1 onion, chopped	1 onion, chopped
2 streaky bacon rashers, chopped	2 fatty bacon slices, chopped
75 g/3 oz cooked ham, chopped	⅓ cup chopped cooked ham
450 g/1 lb fresh spinach	1 lb fresh spinach
pinch of nutmeg	pinch of nutmeg
garlic salt	garlic salt
1 × 2.5 ml spoon/½ teaspoon lemon juice	½ teaspoon lemon juice
225 g/8 oz tomatoes, sliced	½ lb tomatoes, sliced
100 g/4 oz Mozzarella cheese, sliced	¼ lb Mozzarella cheese, sliced
½ × 2.5 ml spoon/¼ teaspoon dried oregano	¼ teaspoon dried oregano

Blend the fresh yeast in the warm milk, or dissolve the sugar in the warm milk and sprinkle the dried yeast on top. Leave the yeast in a warm place for 10 minutes until frothy.

Mix the flour, salt and pepper together then rub (cut) in the butter. Make a well in the centre and pour in the yeast mixture. Stir well until the mixture forms a ball. Knead on a lightly floured surface for 5 minutes. Place dough in an oiled polythene bag and leave in a warm place for 1 hour until doubled in size.

Meanwhile heat the oil in a small saucepan and sauté the onion and bacon for 5 minutes until the onion is soft. Add the cooked ham. Cool. Wash the spinach and cook in the water clinging to the leaves in a covered pan for 3 minutes. Season with nutmeg, garlic salt and lemon juice. Drain thoroughly and cool.

Turn the dough onto a lightly floured board and knead again for 1 minute. Roll out to a 28 cm/11 inch round and place on an oiled baking sheet. Cover the case with the spinach and bacon, onion and ham. Top with the sliced tomatoes and cheese and sprinkle over the oregano. Place in a preheated moderately hot oven (200°C/400°F, Gas Mark 6) and bake for 25 minutes. Serve immediately.
SERVES 6

Wholewheat Pizza

PIZZA WITH SPRATS (SMELTS)

METRIC/IMPERIAL
Base:
225 g/8 oz self-raising flour
salt
50 g/2 oz butter
7 × 15 ml spoons/7
    tablespoons cold water
Topping:
1 × 15 ml spoon/1 tablespoon
    olive oil
1 onion, finely chopped
1 clove garlic, crushed
1 × 227 g/8 oz can tomatoes
1 × 15 ml spoon/1 tablespoon
    tomato purée
1 × 5 ml spoon/1 teaspoon
    dried mixed herbs
salt
freshly ground black pepper
100 g/4 oz mushrooms, sliced
450 g/1 lb sprats, washed and
    drained
100 g/4 oz Cheddar cheese,
    grated

AMERICAN
Base:
2 cups self-rising flour
salt
¼ cup butter
7 tablespoons cold water
Topping:
1 tablespoon olive oil
1 onion, finely chopped
1 clove garlic, crushed
1 × 8 oz can tomatoes
1 tablespoon tomato paste
1 teaspoon dried mixed herbs
salt
freshly ground black pepper
1 cup sliced mushrooms
1 lb smelts, washed and
    drained
1 cup grated Cheddar cheese

Sieve the flour and salt into a bowl and rub (cut) in the butter until the mixture resembles fine breadcrumbs. Add enough cold water to make a soft dough. Roll out on a lightly floured surface to a 30 cm/12 inch round. Place on a greased baking sheet.

Heat the oil in a frying pan (skillet) and sauté the onion and garlic for 7 minutes until golden. Add the tomatoes with their juice, tomato purée (paste), herbs and salt and pepper to taste. Simmer for 5 minutes, then allow to cool. Spread the cooled tomato mixture on the base, then add half the mushrooms. Arrange the sprats (smelts) on top, radiating from the centre. Top with the remaining mushrooms and cheese. Season with salt and pepper.

Place in a preheated moderately hot oven (200°C/400°F, Gas Mark 6) and bake for 35 to 40 minutes until cooked. Serve immediately.

SERVES 4 TO 6

PIZZA FLAN

METRIC/IMPERIAL	AMERICAN
Base:	Base:
175 g/6 oz plain flour	1½ cups all-purpose flour
salt	salt
40 g/1½ oz lard	⅓ cup shortening
40 g/1½ oz margarine	1 egg, beaten
1 egg, beaten	Filling:
Filling:	1 tablespoon olive oil
1 × 15 ml spoon/1 tablespoon olive oil	1 onion, sliced
1 onion, sliced	¼ lb liver sausage
100 g/4 oz liver sausage	½ cup grated Cheddar Cheese
50 g/2 oz Cheddar cheese, grated	¼ lb bratwurst sausage, broiled and cut into strips
100 g/4 oz bratwurst sausage, grilled and cut into strips	2 tomatoes, sliced
2 tomatoes, sliced	¼ teaspoon dried mixed herbs
½ × 2.5 ml spoon/¼ teaspoon dried mixed herbs	

Sieve the flour and salt into a bowl and rub (cut) in the fat until the mixture resembles fine breadcrumbs. Stir in the beaten egg and mix to a dough. Roll out on a lightly floured surface to a 23 cm/9 inch round and fold up the edges.

Heat the oil in a pan and sauté the onion for 5 minutes until soft. Spread the liver sausage over the flan base and cover with the onion and cheese. Arrange the bratwurst and tomato slices on the onions and cheese. Sprinkle with the herbs. Place in a preheated hot oven (220°C/425°F, Gas Mark 7) and bake for 30 minutes. Serve immediately.
SERVES 4

MORTADELLA OMELETTE

METRIC/IMPERIAL	AMERICAN
2 × 15 ml spoons/2 tablespoons olive oil	2 tablespoons olive oil
350 g/12 oz potatoes, coarsely grated	¾ lb potatoes, coarsely grated
1 onion, finely chopped	1 onion, finely chopped
50 g/2 oz stuffed green olives, sliced	½ cup sliced stuffed green olives
2 tomatoes, peeled and chopped	2 tomatoes, skinned and chopped
1 green pepper, seeded and diced	1 green pepper, seeded and diced
100 g/4 oz Mortadella sausage, diced	¼ lb Mortadella sausage, diced
3 eggs	3 eggs
salt	salt
freshly ground black pepper	freshly ground black pepper

Heat the oil in a large frying pan (skillet). Sauté the potatoes and onion for 10 to 15 minutes until the mixture is golden brown. Add the remaining ingredients, except the eggs and salt and pepper, and cook for a further 4 minutes.

Beat the eggs and salt and pepper together and add to the pan. Cook the omelette until set and brown underneath. Invert the omelette onto a plate, slide back into the pan and cook the other side. Serve immediately.
SERVES 4

ITALIAN PANCAKES

METRIC/IMPERIAL	AMERICAN
Filling:	Filling:
40 g/1½ oz butter	3 tablespoons butter
2 onions, chopped	2 onions, chopped
350 g/12 oz minced beef	1½ cups ground beef
1 × 5 ml spoon/1 teaspoon Worcestershire sauce	1 teaspoon Worcestershire sauce
3 × 15 ml spoons/3 tablespoons tomato ketchup	3 tablespoons tomato ketchup
Batter:	Batter:
100 g/4 oz plain flour	1 cup all-purpose flour
salt	salt
1 egg	1 egg
300 ml/½ pint milk	1¼ cups milk
butter for cooking	butter for cooking
Cheese sauce:	Cheese sauce:
25 g/1 oz butter	2 tablespoons butter
25 g/1 oz plain flour	¼ cup all-purpose flour
300 ml/½ pint milk	1¼ cups milk
salt	salt
freshly ground black pepper	freshly ground black pepper
100 g/4 oz grated Cheddar cheese	1 cup grated Cheddar cheese
25 g/1 oz grated Parmesan cheese	¼ cup grated Parmesan cheese

Melt the butter in a saucepan and sauté the onions for 5 minutes until soft. Add the meat and stir until browned. Stir in the Worcestershire sauce and ketchup. Cook, covered for 30 minutes.

Meanwhile, make the pancake batter: sieve the flour and salt into a bowl, add the egg and half the milk and beat until smooth. Gradually stir in the remaining milk. Heat a very little butter in a 20 cm/8 inch frying pan (skillet) and pour in enough batter to make a thin layer over base of the pan. Cook until the underside is golden, then turn to cook other side. Turn onto greaseproof (waxed) paper and keep warm on a plate over a pan of hot water. Make 7 more pancakes.

Divide the filling between the pancakes and roll up. Grease a shallow ovenproof dish and place the pancakes, join downwards in the dish. Keep warm.

To make the cheese sauce: melt the butter in a pan, add the flour and cook for 1 minute. Remove from the heat and gradually stir in the milk. Return to the heat and bring to the boil, stirring. Cook for 1 minute, remove from the heat, add salt, pepper and grated Cheddar cheese, and stir until cheese has melted. Pour the sauce over the pancakes and sprinkle with Parmesan. Brown under a preheated grill (broiler). Serve immediately.

An alternative filling for the pancakes would be spinach and cheese. Fold 250 g/8 oz (1 cup) chopped, cooked and drained spinach with 50 g/2 oz (½ cup) sour cream and 25 g/1 oz (¼ cup) grated Cheddar cheese. Season with freshly ground black pepper and freshly grated nutmeg. Fill the pancakes and place in an ovenproof dish as above. Pour over the cheese sauce and sprinkle with Parmesan. Brown under a preheated grill (broiler). Serve immediately.
SERVES 4

SALAMI AND VEGETABLE OMELETTE

METRIC/IMPERIAL	AMERICAN
40 g/1½ oz butter	3 tablespoons butter
1 small onion, sliced	1 small onion, sliced
1 red pepper, seeded and sliced	1 red pepper, seeded and sliced
175 g/6 oz salami, chopped	6 oz salami, chopped
1 × 213 g/7½ oz can red kidney beans, drained	1 × 7½ oz can red kidney beans, drained
salt	salt
freshly ground black pepper	freshly ground black pepper
4 eggs	4 eggs
1 × 5 ml spoon/1 teaspoon dried mixed herbs	1 teaspoon dried mixed herbs

Melt the butter in a frying pan (skillet) and sauté the onion and pepper for 5 minutes until soft. Stir in the salami, beans and salt and pepper to taste. Heat through.

Lightly beat the eggs together with the herbs and pour over the vegetables. Cook gently, forking up the cooked mixture frequently to let the raw egg mixture run to the bottom of the pan. When nearly firm all over, fold the omelette in half, cut in two and serve immediately.
SERVES 2

Salami and Vegetable Omelette; Noodle Omelette

NOODLE OMELETTE

METRIC/IMPERIAL	AMERICAN
75 g/3 oz noodles	¾ cup noodles
salt	salt
2 eggs, beaten	2 eggs, beaten
freshly ground black pepper	freshly ground black pepper
pinch of nutmeg	pinch of nutmeg
40 g/1½ oz butter	3 tablespoons butter
1 small onion, sliced	1 small onion, sliced
2 tomatoes, peeled and sliced	2 tomatoes, skinned and sliced
1 × 5 cm/2 inch piece cucumber, peeled and sliced	1 × 2 inch piece cucumber, peeled and sliced
75 g/3 oz Cheddar cheese, grated	¾ cup grated Cheddar cheese

Cook the noodles in a large pan of boiling salted water for 10 minutes. Drain and cool. Mix the noodles with the eggs, salt, pepper and nutmeg to taste.

Melt half the butter in an 18 cm/7 inch frying pan (skillet) and sauté the onion for 5 minutes until soft. Add the tomatoes, and cucumber and cook gently for 1 minute. Remove from the pan and keep hot.

Melt the remaining butter in the pan and pour in the egg and noodle mixture. Cook the omelette until set and brown underneath. Place the cooked onion, tomatoes and cucumber on top, season with salt and pepper and sprinkle over the grated cheese. Place under a preheated hot grill (broiler) until lightly browned. Serve immediately.
SERVES 2

SAVOURY MUSHROOM TART

METRIC/IMPERIAL	AMERICAN
225 g/8 oz frozen puff pastry	½ lb frozen puff paste
450 g/1 lb macaroni	4 cups macaroni
salt	salt
175 g/6 oz chicken livers, chopped	6 oz chicken livers, chopped
2 × 15 ml spoons/2 tablespoons olive oil	2 tablespoons olive oil
225 g/8 oz mushrooms, sliced	2 cups sliced mushrooms
2 onions, thinly sliced	2 onions, thinly sliced
4 eggs, beaten	4 eggs, beaten
freshly ground black pepper	freshly ground black pepper
50 g/2 oz grated Parmesan cheese	½ cup grated Parmesan cheese
25 g/1 oz butter	2 tablespoons butter

Roll out the pastry (paste) and use to line a 1.2 litre/2 pint pie dish. Cook the macaroni in a large pan of boiling salted water for 10 minutes until tender. Drain thoroughly and add the chopped chicken livers.

Heat the oil in a saucepan and sauté the mushrooms and onions for 5 minutes until soft. Add to the macaroni mixture with the eggs. Add salt and pepper to taste and pour into the lined pie dish. Cover with grated Parmesan cheese and dot with butter. Place in a preheated hot oven (220°C/425°F, Gas Mark 7) and bake for 30 to 40 minutes, or until top is well browned. Serve immediately, or warm.

SERVES 4 TO 6

WHOLEWHEAT MORTADELLA SCONES

METRIC/IMPERIAL	AMERICAN
100 g/4 oz self-raising flour	1 cup self-rising flour
100 g/4 oz wholewheat flour	1 cup wholewheat flour
1½ × 5 ml spoons/1½ teaspoons baking powder	1½ teaspoons baking powder
50 g/2 oz butter	¼ cup butter
50 g/2 oz Mortadella sausage, diced	¼ cup diced Mortadella sausage
150 ml/¼ pint milk	⅔ cup milk

Mix the flours and baking powder together. Rub (cut) in the butter and mix in the Mortadella. Pour in the milk and mix lightly to form a fairly soft dough. Roll out on a lightly floured surface to 1 cm/½ inch thickness.

Using a 5 cm/2 inch cutter, cut out approximately 12 scones. Place on a greased baking sheet and brush with milk. Place in a preheated hot oven (220°C/425°F, Gas Mark 7) and bake for 10 to 12 minutes. Serve warm.

MAKES 12

FOCACCIA

METRIC/IMPERIAL	AMERICAN
25 g/1 oz fresh yeast, or 15 g/½ oz dried yeast and 1 × 5 ml spoon/1 teaspoon sugar	1 cake compressed yeast, or 1 tablespoon dried yeast and 1 teaspoon sugar
450 ml/¾ pint warm water	2 cups warm water
1 kg/2 lb strong plain white flour	8 cups strong all-purpose white flour
salt	salt
150 ml/¼ pint olive oil	⅔ cup olive oil
3 onions, thinly sliced	3 onions, thinly sliced
1 egg	1 egg
100 g/4 oz black olives	¾ cup ripe olives

Blend the fresh yeast in 150 ml/¼ pint (⅔ cup) warm water, or dissolve the sugar in the same amount of warm water and sprinkle the dried yeast on top. Leave the yeast in a warm place for 10 minutes until frothy.

Sieve 225 g/8 oz (2 cups) flour into a bowl with the salt. Make a well in the centre and pour in the yeast mixture and 3 × 15 ml spoons/3 tablespoons oil. Mix to a soft dough. Knead on a lightly floured surface for 5 minutes. Place dough in a large oiled polythene bag and leave in a warm place for 1 hour until doubled in size.

Meanwhile, heat 3 × 15 ml spoons/3 tablespoons oil and sauté onions for 5 minutes until soft. Allow to cool.

When the dough has doubled in size, sieve the remaining flour into a separate bowl, make a well in the centre and add the egg, remaining 4 × 15 ml spoons/4 tablespoons oil and remaining 300 ml/½ pint (1¼ cups) warm water. Mix well together then add the risen dough. Turn out onto a floured board and knead for 5 minutes. Return to the oiled bag and leave to rise for 45 minutes.

Divide dough in half. Roll to a 5 mm/¼ inch thickness and use to line two baking sheets 30 × 23 cm/12 × 9 inches. Spread over the cooked onions and oil. Add the olives and brush generously with extra oil. Place in a preheated hot oven (220°C/425°F, Gas Mark 7) and bake for 30 minutes. Serve hot or cold.

MAKES 16 SLICES

CROSTINI

METRIC/IMPERIAL	AMERICAN
8 small round slices bread	8 small round slices bread
8 slices Cheddar or Bel Paese cheese	8 slices Cheddar or Bel Paese cheese
1 × 50 g/1¾ oz can anchovies	1 × 2 oz can anchovies
50 g/2 oz olives, sliced	½ cup sliced olives.

Toast the bread on both sides under a preheated hot grill (broiler). Place slices of cheese on top and grill (broil) until just melted. Remove from the heat and arrange strips of anchovy and sliced olives on top. Serve immediately.

SERVES 4

Focaccia; Wholewheat Mortadella Scones

POULTRY AND GAME

STUFFED CHICKEN BREASTS

METRIC/IMPERIAL	AMERICAN
4 chicken breasts, skinned and boned	4 chicken breasts, skinned and boned
salt	salt
freshly ground black pepper	freshly ground black pepper
4 thin small slices cooked ham	4 thin small slices processed ham
4 thin slices Bel Paese cheese	4 thin slices Bel Paese cheese
4 cooked or canned asparagus spears	4 cooked or canned asparagus spears
flour for dusting	flour for dusting
40 g/1½ oz butter	3 tablespoons butter
1 × 15 ml spoon/1 tablespoon oil	1 tablespoon oil
6 × 15 ml spoons/6 tablespoons Marsala	6 tablespoons Marsala
2 × 15 ml spoons/2 tablespoons chicken stock	2 tablespoons chicken bouillon
cooked or canned asparagus spears to garnish	cooked or canned asparagus spears to garnish

Lay the chicken breasts flat between pieces of damp greaseproof (waxed) paper and beat with a rolling pin until thin. Season with salt and pepper and place a slice of ham on each, then a slice of cheese and an asparagus spear. Roll each breast up carefully, wind a piece of cotton around to hold it, and dust with flour.

Heat 25 g/1 oz (2 tablespoons) of the butter and the oil in a frying pan (skillet) and sauté the chicken rolls over a very low heat, turning frequently, for about 15 minutes until tender and golden. Remove the cotton, transfer the rolls to a warm serving dish and keep warm.

Add the Marsala, stock (bouillon) and remaining butter to the juices in the pan, bring to the boil and simmer for 3 to 4 minutes, scraping up the juices from the base of the pan. Spoon sauce over the chicken and garnish with asparagus spears. Serve immediately.

SERVES 4

CHICKEN WITH EGG AND LEMON SAUCE

METRIC/IMPERIAL	AMERICAN
1 kg/2 lb chicken	2 lb chicken
1 small onion, sliced	1 small onion, sliced
1 small carrot, sliced	1 small carrot, sliced
1 small celery stick, sliced	1 small celery stalk, sliced
1 bay leaf	1 bay leaf
4 whole peppercorns	4 whole peppercorns
salt	salt
freshly ground black pepper	freshly ground black pepper
2 × 15 ml spoons/2 tablespoons oil	2 tablespoons oil
25 g/1 oz butter	2 tablespoons butter
25 g/1 oz flour	¼ cup flour
2 egg yolks	2 egg yolks
juice of ½ large lemon	juice of ½ large lemon
To garnish:	To garnish:
2 × 15 ml spoons/2 tablespoons chopped parsley	2 tablespoons chopped parsley

Remove the giblets from the chicken and put into a saucepan with the onion, carrot, celery, bay leaf, peppercorns and salt. Cover with cold water, bring to the boil, cover and simmer gently for 30 minutes, then strain the stock (bouillon) and reserve 300 ml/½ pint (1¼ cups).

Divide the chicken into 4 portions, and season with salt and pepper. Heat the oil and butter in a large frying pan (skillet) over a low heat and sauté the chicken pieces gently, turning occasionally, for about 15 minutes until golden brown. Lift out the chicken and transfer to a plate.

Sprinkle the flour into the pan, stir and cook for 1 minute, then gradually stir in the reserved stock (bouillon). Bring to the boil, stirring, return the chicken to the pan, cover tightly and simmer for 30 to 40 minutes. Lift out the chicken and arrange on a warm serving dish.

Skim off any surface fat from the chicken sauce. Put the egg yolks and lemon juice into a small basin, add 2 × 15 ml spoons/2 tablespoons of the chicken sauce and beat lightly. Stir into the chicken sauce and heat, without boiling, until just thickened. Adjust the seasoning, pour the sauce over the chicken and garnish with parsley. Serve immediately.

SERVES 4

SAUTÉED CHICKEN WITH OLIVES

METRIC/IMPERIAL	AMERICAN
1.75 kg/4 lb chicken, cut into 6 portions	4 lb chicken, cut into 6 portions
seasoned flour for coating	seasoned flour for coating
3 × 15 ml spoons/3 tablespoons olive oil	3 tablespoons olive oil
1 large onion, chopped	1 large onion, chopped
1–2 cloves garlic, crushed	1–2 cloves garlic, crushed
1 bay leaf	1 bay leaf
150 ml/¼ pint dry white wine	⅔ cup dry white wine
1 × 400 g/14 oz can peeled tomatoes	1 × 14 oz can skinned tomatoes
1 × 15 ml spoon/1 tablespoon tomato purée	1 tablespoon tomato paste
12 black olives	12 ripe olives
freshly ground black pepper	freshly ground black pepper
salt (optional)	salt (optional)
parsley to garnish	parsley to garnish

Wash and dry the chicken portions and dust lightly with seasoned flour. Heat the oil in a large heavy based saucepan and sauté the chicken until golden all over. Transfer to a plate. Add the onion to the pan and sauté for 5 minutes until soft. Add the garlic and bay leaf and sauté for 1 minute. Pour in the wine and simmer for 1 to 2 minutes, then add the tomatoes and their juice and the tomato purée (paste). Bring to the boil, breaking up the tomatoes if whole, return the chicken to the pan and add the olives. Cover the pan and simmer gently, stirring occasionally, for 45 minutes or until the chicken is tender.

Transfer the chicken to a warm serving dish. Boil the sauce rapidly, uncovered, until reduced by half. Remove the bay leaf, adjust the salt and pour the sauce over the chicken. Garnish with parsley and serve immediately.
SERVES 6

Sautéed Chicken with Olives

CHICKEN TONNATO

METRIC/IMPERIAL	AMERICAN
4 chicken breasts, skinned and boned	4 chicken breasts, skinned and boned
600 ml/1 pint chicken stock	2½ cups chicken bouillon
1 onion, halved	1 onion, halved
1 celery stick, roughly chopped	1 celery stalk, roughly chopped
salt	salt
freshly ground black pepper	freshly ground black pepper
pinch of dried thyme	pinch of dried thyme
few parsley stalks	few parsley stalks
½ bay leaf	½ bay leaf
150 ml/¼ pint white wine (optional)	⅔ cup white wine (optional)
Sauce:	Sauce:
450 ml/¾ pint thick mayonnaise	2 cups thick mayonnaise
1 × 198 g/7 oz can tuna, drained	1 × 7 oz can tuna, drained
6 anchovy fillets, drained	6 anchovy fillets, drained
2 × 15 ml spoons/2 tablespoons lemon juice	2 tablespoons lemon juice
3 × 15 ml spoons/3 tablespoons drained capers	3 tablespoons drained capers
To garnish:	To garnish:
anchovy fillets	anchovy fillets
capers	capers
tomato slices	tomato slices

Place the chicken, stock (bouillon), onion, celery, salt and pepper to taste, herbs, wine, if using, and enough water to cover, in a large saucepan. Bring to the boil, then simmer very gently for 20 to 30 minutes until the chicken is tender and cooked. Remove the chicken from the pan with a slotted spoon and leave to cool.

To make the sauce: purée the mayonnaise, tuna, anchovy fillets, lemon juice and capers in a blender until smooth. Put the cooled chicken breasts on a serving dish and spoon the sauce over them to cover. Garnish with anchovy fillets, capers and tomato slices. Serve immediately.
SERVES 4

CHARCOAL GRILLED (BROILED) CHICKEN

METRIC/IMPERIAL	AMERICAN
1 × 1.25 kg/2½ lb chicken, halved	1 × 2½ lb chicken, halved
7 × 15 ml spoons/7 tablespoons olive oil	7 tablespoons olive oil
salt	salt
freshly ground black pepper	freshly ground black pepper
1 lemon, sliced, to serve	1 lemon, sliced, to serve

Beat the chicken halves lightly with a mallet, taking care not to break the bones.

Rub the chicken with the oil and sprinkle with salt and pepper. Cook for about 40 minutes over a charcoal grill (broiler) until the skin is crisp and crunchy and the meat is tender. Garnish with the lemon and serve immediately.
SERVES 4

Chicken Tonnato

CHICKEN CACCIATORE

METRIC/IMPERIAL	AMERICAN
1 × 1.5 kg/3 lb chicken	1 × 3 lb chicken
3 × 15 ml spoons/3 tablespoons olive oil	3 tablespoons olive oil
2 onions, chopped	2 onions, chopped
1 clove garlic, chopped	1 clove garlic, chopped
450 g/1 lb tomatoes, peeled and chopped	2 cups skinned, chopped tomatoes
225 g/8 oz mushrooms, sliced	2 cups sliced mushrooms
1 bay leaf	1 bay leaf
pinch of rosemary	pinch of rosemary
200 ml/⅓ pint red wine	1 cup red wine
salt	salt
freshly ground black pepper	freshly ground black pepper
sprigs of rosemary to garnish	sprigs of rosemary to garnish

Divide the chicken into 4 portions. Heat the oil in a heavy pan. Add the onions and garlic and sauté for 7 minutes until golden. Remove the onion and garlic and increase the heat. Brown the chicken on all sides in the oil. Return the onion to the pan and add the tomatoes, mushrooms, herbs and wine.

Lower the heat, season well with salt and pepper to taste and cook very gently for about 1 hour, turning the chicken occasionally. Garnish with rosemary and serve immediately.
SERVES 4

SPIT-ROASTED CHICKEN

METRIC/IMPERIAL	AMERICAN
1 × 1.5 kg/3 lb chicken	1 × 3 lb chicken
7 × 15 ml spoons/7 tablespoons olive oil	7 tablespoons olive oil
few sage leaves, chopped	few sage leaves, chopped
1 sprig of rosemary, chopped	1 sprig of rosemary, chopped
225 g/8 oz raw ham or bacon rashers	½ lb raw ham or bacon slices
2 cloves garlic, crushed	2 cloves garlic, crushed
salt	salt
freshly ground black pepper	freshly ground black pepper

Brush the chicken with the oil, then sprinkle with half the sage and rosemary. Leave to stand in a cool place for 2 hours.

Chop half the ham or bacon and mix with the garlic, remaining sage and rosemary, and salt and pepper to taste. Stuff the chicken with the ham mixture and secure opening with trussing thread or string.

Wrap the chicken in the remaining slices of ham or bacon, then tie them on with more thread or string. Thread the chicken on a spit and spit roast for 1¼ hours until the skin is crunchy and the meat is tender. Alternatively, place in a preheated moderately hot oven (200°C/400°F, Gas Mark 6) and cook for 1¼ hours or until tender. Serve immediately.
SERVES 4

PRESSED CHICKEN

METRIC/IMPERIAL	AMERICAN
1 × 1 kg/2 lb chicken	1 × 2 lb chicken
3 × 15 ml spoons/3 tablespoons olive oil	3 tablespoons olive oil
1 clove garlic, crushed	1 clove garlic, crushed
1 bay leaf, crumbled	1 bay leaf, crumbled
1 sprig of rosemary	1 sprig of rosemary
salt	salt
freshly ground black pepper	freshly ground black pepper
juice of ½ lemon	juice of ½ lemon

Cut the chicken in half along the backbone. Remove the backbone and beat the chicken with a mallet as flat as possible. Wash and dry the chicken with kitchen paper towels. Place flat in a shallow dish. Mix all the remaining ingredients, except the lemon juice, and pour over the chicken. Leave to marinate for 2 to 3 hours, turning once.

Oil the base of a heavy frying pan (skillet) and heat gently. Put in the chicken and press a heavy lid with fits inside the pan down on top of it. Cook over low to moderate heat for 30 to 40 minutes, until the chicken is golden brown and tender. Transfer to a warm serving dish.

Sprinkle the lemon juice over the chicken together with any juices from the chicken. Serve immediately.

SERVES 2

WOOD PIGEONS WITH PEAS

METRIC/IMPERIAL	AMERICAN
4 young pigeons	4 young pigeons
salt	salt
freshly ground black pepper	freshly ground black pepper
25 g/1 oz butter	2 tablespoons butter
2 × 15 ml spoons/2 tablespoons oil	2 tablespoons oil
1 medium onion, chopped	1 medium onion, chopped
5 streaky bacon rashers, diced	5 fatty bacon slices, diced
150 ml/¼ pint dry white wine	⅔ cup dry white wine
300 ml/½ pint chicken stock	1¼ cups chicken bouillon
450 g/1 lb shelled green peas	3 cups shelled green peas
1 × 5 ml spoon/1 teaspoon sugar	1 teaspoon sugar

Wash and dry the pigeons with kitchen paper towels. Season inside and out with salt and pepper

Heat the butter and oil in a large heavy based saucepan. Sauté the onion and bacon for 5 minutes until the onion is soft. Increase the heat, add the pigeons and cook, turning frequently, for about 15 minutes, until golden brown all over.

Add the wine and allow to bubble briskly until reduced to half the quantity. Add the stock (bouillon), bring to the boil, cover and simmer very gently for 1¼ to 1½ hours, or until the pigeons are almost tender. Check the pan from time to time to make sure there is enough liquid, adding more stock (bouillon) if necessary.

Stir in the peas with the sugar and a little salt, cover and simmer gently for another 20 minutes, or until the peas and pigeons are tender. Transfer to a warm serving dish and serve immediately.

SERVES 4

DUCK IN SWEET-SOUR SAUCE

METRIC/IMPERIAL	AMERICAN
1 × 2.25 kg/5 lb duckling	1 × 5 lb duckling
salt	salt
freshly ground black pepper	freshly ground black pepper
25 g/1 oz plain flour	¼ cup all-purpose flour
2 × 15 ml spoons/2 tablespoons olive oil	2 tablespoons olive oil
2 large onions, thinly sliced	2 large onions, thinly sliced
½ × 2.5 ml spoon/¼ teaspoon ground cloves	¼ teaspoon ground cloves
600 ml/1 pint well flavoured duckling stock made from the giblets	2½ cups well-flavoured duckling bouillon, made from the giblets
2 × 15 ml spoons/2 tablespoons finely chopped fresh mint or 2 × 5 ml spoons/2 teaspoons dried mint	2 tablespoons finely chopped fresh mint or 2 teaspoons dried mint
75 g/3 oz sultanas	½ cup raisins
50 g/2 oz sugar	¼ cup sugar
4 × 15 ml spoons/4 tablespoons water	4 tablespoons water
2 × 15 ml spoons/2 tablespoons wine vinegar	2 tablespoons wine vinegar
sprigs of mint to garnish	sprigs of mint to garnish

Wash the duckling and pat dry inside and out with kitchen paper towels. Season well with salt and pepper and dredge well with the flour.

Heat the oil in a large heavy based saucepan. Sauté the onions for 5 minutes until soft. Add the duckling and cook, turning until browned all over. Sprinkle with ground cloves. Pour in the strained stock (bouillon), bring slowly to the boil then reduce the heat. Cover and simmer gently for 1½ hours or until tender. Carefully remove duck from pan, divide into 4 portions and arrange on a warm serving dish. Keep hot.

Skim the fat from the liquid in the pan then stir in the mint and sultanas (raisins). Meanwhile heat the sugar and water in a small heavy based pan until it turns deep golden brown. Stir this into the mint sauce, taking care as it will splutter a little at first. Stir in the vinegar and simmer for 5 to 10 minutes, uncovered, until the sauce is reduced to a syrupy consistency. Pour the sauce over the duck and garnish with sprigs of mint. Serve immediately.

SERVES 4

Wood Pigeons with Peas; Pressed Chicken

DUCKLING WITH OLIVES

METRIC/IMPERIAL
1 × 2.25 kg/5 lb duckling
salt
Sauce:
2 streaky bacon rashers,
    chopped
1 carrot, thinly sliced
1 small onion, finely chopped
1 clove garlic, crushed
1 celery stick, chopped
25 g/1 oz plain flour
300 ml/½ pint well-flavoured
    duckling stock, made from
    the giblets
2 × 15 ml spoons/2
    tablespoons tomato purée
1 × 2.5 ml spoon/½ teaspoon
    dried basil
salt
freshly ground black pepper
150 ml/¼ pint white wine
2 large green olives, stoned
    and sliced
12 black olives, stoned and
    sliced
To garnish:
pared lemon rind
few whole green and black
    olives

AMERICAN
1 × 5 lb duckling
salt
Sauce:
2 fatty bacon slices, chopped
1 carrot, thinly sliced
1 small onion, finely chopped
1 clove garlic, crushed
1 celery stalk, chopped
¼ cup all-purpose flour
1¼ cups well-flavoured
    duckling bouillon, made
    from the giblets
2 tablespoons tomato paste
½ teaspoon dried basil
salt
freshly ground black pepper
⅔ cup white wine
2 large pitted green olives,
    sliced
12 pitted ripe olives, sliced
To garnish:
pared lemon zest
few whole green and ripe
    olives.

Wash the duckling and pat dry inside and out with kitchen paper towels. Prick the skin all over with a fork and rub with salt. Place the duckling, breast uppermost and uncovered on a wire rack in a roasting pan in the centre of a preheated moderate oven (180°C/350°F, Gas Mark 4), and roast for 2½ hours.

Meanwhile prepare the sauce: heat 2 × 15 ml spoons/2 tablespoons of duckling dripping (taken from the roasting duck) in a saucepan. Add the bacon and fry for 2 to 3 minutes until lightly browned. Add the carrot, onion, garlic and celery and sauté for a further 5 minutes. Sprinkle in the flour, mix well and continue to sauté until lightly browned. Remove from the heat and gradually blend in the strained stock (bouillon) and tomato purée (paste). Stir in the basil. Return to the heat and stir until the sauce thickens. Season well with salt and pepper to taste. Reduce heat and simmer very gently for 1 hour, stirring from time to time to prevent sticking.

Press the prepared sauce through a sieve into a clean, small roasting tin (pan). Stir in the white wine and olives. Cut the roast duckling into 4 portions and add to the pan, spooning a little sauce over each portion. Return to a preheated moderately hot oven (200°C/400°F, Gas Mark 6) and cook for 20 minutes or until heated through.

Arrange the duckling on a warm serving dish with the sauce. Sprinkle with lemon rind (zest) and garnish with green and black olives. Serve immediately.
SERVES 4

TURKEY FILLETS LIMONE

METRIC/IMPERIAL	AMERICAN
4 turkey fillets or escalopes	4 turkey cutlets
salt	salt
freshly ground black pepper	freshly ground black pepper
75 g/3 oz butter	1/3 cup butter
2 onions, finely chopped	2 onions, finely chopped
100 g/4 oz mushrooms, sliced	1 cup sliced mushrooms
40 g/1½ oz plain flour	6 tablespoons all-purpose flour
450 ml/¾ pint chicken stock	2 cups chicken bouillon
grated rind and juice of 1 lemon	grated zest and juice of 1 lemon
1 × 15 ml spoon/1 tablespoon chopped parsley	1 tablespoon chopped parsley
50 g/2 oz chopped gherkins (optional)	1/3 cup chopped gherkins (optional)
4 × 15 ml spoons/4 tablespoons double cream (optional)	1/4 cup heavy cream (optional)

Season the turkey with salt and pepper. Melt the butter in a frying pan (skillet) and sauté the onions for 5 minutes until soft. Add the turkey and sauté lightly on each side to seal, then remove from the pan.

Add the mushrooms to the pan and sauté for a further 1 minute. Stir in the flour and cook for 1 minute. Add the stock (bouillon) and lemon rind (zest) and juice and bring to the boil. Stir in the parsley and gherkins, if using, and return the turkey to the pan. Cover and simmer gently for about 30 minutes, turning once or twice, until tender. Adjust seasoning and stir in the cream, if using. Transfer to a warm serving dish and serve immediately.

SERVES 4

Turkey Ripieno

TURKEY RIPIENO

METRIC/IMPERIAL	AMERICAN
1 × 4.5 kg/10 lb turkey	1 × 10 lb turkey
salt	salt
freshly ground black pepper	freshly ground black pepper
melted butter for basting	melted butter for basting
parsley to garnish	parsley to garnish
Stuffing:	Stuffing:
450 g/1 lb chestnuts	1 lb chestnuts
40 g/1½ oz butter	3 tablespoons butter
2 streaky bacon rashers, chopped	2 fatty bacon slices, chopped
175 g/6 oz pork sausage meat	¾ cup pork sausage meat
8 large prunes, soaked overnight, stoned and chopped	8 large prunes, soaked overnight, pitted and chopped
2 ripe pears, peeled and chopped	2 ripe pears, skinned and chopped
2 × 15 ml spoons/2 tablespoons brandy or dry white vermouth	2 tablespoons brandy or dry white vermouth

Remove the giblets from the turkey. Chop the liver and reserve. Wash the turkey and pat dry inside and out with kitchen paper towels. Season inside and out with salt and pepper.

To make the stuffing: cut a cross on the pointed end of each chestnut. Place the chestnuts in a pan, cover with water and simmer for 15 minutes. Drain, and while still hot, peel off the shells and inner skins. Chop the chestnuts roughly. Melt the butter in a saucepan, fry the bacon for 1 to 2 minutes, then stir in the liver, chestnuts, sausage meat, prunes, pears, brandy or vermouth and salt and pepper to taste. Cool, then stuff loosely into the neck end of the turkey, putting any remaining stuffing into the body cavity. Secure the opening with trussing thread or string.

Stand the turkey on a rack in a roasting tin (pan), brush all over with melted butter and cover loosely with foil. Place in the centre of a preheated moderate oven (180°C/350°F, Gas Mark 4) and roast for 1 hour. Lower the temperature to 160°C/325°F, Gas Mark 3 and cook for a further 2½ to 3 hours, removing the foil for the last 30 minutes of cooking time. Transfer to a warm serving plate and garnish with parsley. Serve immediately.
SERVES 12 TO 15

TURKEY WITH CAPERS

METRIC/IMPERIAL	AMERICAN
2 turkey breasts, halved lengthwise	2 turkey breasts, halved lengthwise
salt	salt
freshly ground black pepper	freshly ground black pepper
4 × 15 ml spoons/4 tablespoons oil	¼ cup oil
40 g/1½ oz plain flour	6 tablespoons all-purpose flour
300 ml/½ pint single cream	1¼ cups light cream
150 ml/¼ pint white wine	⅔ cup white wine
1 × 15 ml spoon/1 tablespoon finely grated lemon rind	1 tablespoon finely grated lemon zest
1 × 5 ml spoon/1 teaspoon fresh thyme or 1 × 2.5 ml spoon/½ teaspoon dried thyme	1 teaspoon fresh thyme or ½ teaspoon dried thyme
½ × 2.5 ml spoon/¼ teaspoon dried marjoram	¼ teaspoon dried marjoram
2 × 15 ml spoons/2 tablespoons capers	2 tablespoons capers
To garnish:	To garnish:
few strips of thinly pared lemon rind	few strips of thinly pared lemon zest
watercress	watercress

Rub the turkey with salt and pepper. Heat the oil in a frying pan (skillet) over moderate heat and sauté the turkey gently for 4 to 5 minutes on each side until lightly browned. Remove and place in an ovenproof dish.

Stir the flour into the pan juices and cook for 1 minute, then gradually stir in the cream and wine. Bring the sauce to just below boiling point, stirring continuously, then lower the heat and simmer for 2 minutes. Add the remaining ingredients and pour over the turkey. Cover and place in a preheated moderate oven (180°C/350°F, Gas Mark 4). Cook for 15 minutes or until the turkey is tender. Taste and adjust the seasoning, if necessary.

Garnish with strips of lemon rind (zest) and watercress. Serve immediately.
SERVES 4

TURKEY SALTIMBOCCA

METRIC/IMPERIAL	AMERICAN
4 turkey breast fillets, skinned and boned	4 turkey breast fillets, skinned and boned
flour	flour
4 slices lean ham	4 slices lean ham
50 g/2 oz Cheddar cheese, grated	½ cup grated Cheddar cheese
50 g/2 oz grated Parmesan cheese	½ cup grated Parmesan cheese
3 × 15 ml spoons/3 tablespoons olive oil	3 tablespoons olive oil
3 tomatoes, peeled and finely diced	3 tomatoes, skinned and finely diced
50 g/2 oz walnuts, roughly chopped	½ cup roughly chopped walnuts
chopped parsley to garnish	chopped parsley to garnish

Lay the turkey breasts flat between pieces of damp grease-proof (waxed) paper, and beat with a rolling pin until thin. Dust each of the breasts with flour then place a slice of ham on each, trimming the edges to fit the turkey. Mix the cheeses together and sprinkle a little over the ham, and then roll up with the turkey meat on the outside.

Heat the oil in a frying pan (skillet) and sauté turkey rolls until golden brown on the outside and cooked through. Place on a grill (broiler) tray and sprinkle with the remaining cheese, then with the diced tomato and walnuts. Place under a preheated hot grill (broiler) until the cheese melts. Transfer to a warm serving dish, garnish with the parsley and serve immediately.

SERVES 4

LOMBARDY RABBIT STEW

METRIC/IMPERIAL	AMERICAN
8 × 15 ml/8 tablespoons oil	8 tablespoons oil
1 onion, chopped	1 onion, chopped
1 carrot, chopped	1 carrot, chopped
750 g/1½ lb tomatoes, peeled and chopped	3 cups skinned, chopped tomatoes
1 bay leaf	1 bay leaf
600 ml/1 pint chicken stock	2½ cups chicken bouillon
sugar	sugar
salt	salt
40 g/1½ oz plain flour	6 tablespoons all-purpose flour
3 × 15 ml spoons/3 tablespoons milk	3 tablespoons milk
4 rabbit portions	4 rabbit portions

Heat half the oil in a large heavy saucepan. Sauté the onion and carrot for 5 minutes until soft. Add the tomatoes, bay leaf and stock (bouillon). Cover and simmer for 20 minutes. Strain and season with sugar and salt to taste. Mix flour and milk together until smooth and add to the sauce. Bring to the boil, stirring. Remove from the heat.

Heat the remaining oil in a frying pan (skillet). Sauté the rabbit portions until browned all over. Transfer with a slotted spoon to the sauce. Cover and cook gently for about 1½ hours. Transfer to a warm serving dish and serve immediately.

SERVES 4

RABBIT WITH OLIVES

METRIC/IMPERIAL	AMERICAN
7 × 15 ml spoons/7 tablespoons olive oil	7 tablespoons olive oil
1 × 1.25 kg/2½ lb rabbit, cut into serving pieces	1 × 2½ lb rabbit, cut into serving pieces
2 cloves garlic, crushed	2 cloves garlic, crushed
1 sprig of rosemary, chopped	1 sprig of rosemary, chopped
200 ml/⅓ pint red wine	1 cup red wine
salt	salt
freshly ground black pepper	freshly ground black pepper
6–8 × 15 ml spoons/6–8 tablespoons chicken stock	6–8 tablespoons chicken bouillon
2 tomatoes, peeled and chopped	2 tomatoes, skinned and chopped
225 g/8 oz black olives, halved and stoned	½ lb pitted and halved ripe olives

Heat the oil in a large heavy based saucepan. Add the rabbit sprinkled with garlic and rosemary. Sauté gently until the rabbit is brown on all sides, turning frequently. Add the wine and season to taste. Cover and simmer for 30 minutes, adding stock (bouillon) to moisten as necessary. Add the tomatoes and olives and cook for a further 40 minutes until the rabbit is tender. Transfer to a warm serving dish and serve immediately

SERVES 4

HARE WITH SAUSAGES

METRIC/IMPERIAL	AMERICAN
50 g/2 oz butter	¼ cup butter
1 small onion, chopped	1 small onion, chopped
4 streaky bacon rashers	4 fatty bacon slices, chopped
1 × 1.5 kg/3 lb hare, cut into serving pieces	1 × 3 lb hare, cut into serving pieces
300 ml/½ pint chicken stock	1¼ cups chicken bouillon
Sauce:	Sauce:
5 × 15 ml spoons/5 tablespoons olive oil	5 tablespoons olive oil
175 g/6 oz Italian sausage, chopped	6 oz Italian sausage, chopped
1 hare or chicken liver, chopped	1 hare or chicken liver, chopped
300 ml/½ pint chicken stock	1¼ cups chicken bouillon
4 × 15 ml spoons/4 tablespoons chopped parsley	4 tablespoons chopped parsley
salt	salt
freshly ground black pepper	freshly ground black pepper
juice of ½ lemon	juice of ½ lemon

Melt the butter in a large heavy based saucepan. Sauté the onion and bacon for 5 minutes. Add the hare and stock (bouillon). Bring to the boil, cover and simmer gently for 2 hours.

To make the sauce: heat the oil in a heavy based pan, add the sausage and liver and sauté gently for 5 minutes. Add the stock, parsley and salt and pepper to taste. Simmer for 30 minutes until the sauce thickens. Stir in the lemon juice and add to the hare 10 minutes before serving. Transfer to a warm serving dish and serve immediately.

SERVES 4

Rabbit with Olives

FISH

RICE AND SHELLFISH SALAD

METRIC/IMPERIAL	AMERICAN
Rice salad:	Rice salad:
225 g/8 oz Italian rice	1 cup Italian rice
5 × 15 ml spoons/5 tablespoons olive oil	1/3 cup olive oil
1 × 15 ml spoon/1 tablespoon lemon juice	1 tablespoon lemon juice
1 × 15 ml spoon/1 tablespoon wine vinegar	1 tablespoon wine vinegar
salt	salt
freshly ground black pepper	freshly ground black pepper
1 × 15 ml spoon/1 tablespoon grated onion	1 tablespoon grated onion
1 large fennel root, shredded	1 large fennel root, shredded
2 × 15 ml spoons/2 tablespoons chopped parsley	2 tablespoons chopped parsley
Shellfish:	Shellfish:
1.2 litres/2 pints mussels	5 cups mussels
1.2 litres/2 pints clams	5 cups clams
450 g/1 lb cooked unshelled prawns or scampi	1 lb cooked unshelled shrimp or jumbo shrimp
To garnish:	To garnish:
fennel leaves	fennel leaves
2 hard-boiled eggs, quartered	2 hard-cooked eggs, quartered
black olives (optional)	ripe olives (optional)

Cook the rice in a large saucepan of boiling salted water until just tender. Drain thoroughly, put into a bowl and add the oil, lemon juice, vinegar, salt, pepper and onion. Toss lightly until well mixed and set aside until cold. Fold the fennel into the rice with the parsley. Adjust the seasoning.

Cover the mussels with cold water, discarding any which are open or float to the top. Scrub the mussels to remove any barnacles and remove the beards. Soak in fresh cold water. Drain. Put into a wide saucepan, cover and place over moderately high heat for about 5 minutes, shaking the pan frequently until the mussels begin to open. As they open, transfer them to a colander. Discard any mussels that do not open.

When cool remove most of the mussels from their shells, leave a few unshelled for garnishing.

Prepare and cook the clams in the same way. Shell most of the clams and prawns (shrimp) or scampi (jumbo shrimp), reserving a few of each for garnishing.

Fold the cold shellfish into the rice and pile into the centre of a serving dish. Top with a few unshelled prawns (shrimp) and fennel leaves. Garnish with the eggs, olives, if using, and the reserved shellfish. Serve immediately.
SERVES 4

SARDINIAN SEAFOOD SALAD

METRIC/IMPERIAL	AMERICAN
225 g/8 oz wholewheat macaroni	1/2 lb wholewheat macaroni
salt	salt
25 g/1 oz butter	2 tablespoons butter
50 g/2 oz mushrooms	2 oz mushrooms
100 g/4 oz cooked and shelled mussels	1/2 cup cooked and shelled mussels
100 g/4 oz peeled prawns	2/3 cup shelled shrimp
1 × 50 g/1¾ oz can anchovies, drained	1 × 2 oz can anchovies, drained
3 tomatoes, cut into wedges	3 tomatoes, cut into wedges
Dressing:	Dressing:
5 × 15 ml spoons/5 tablespoons olive oil	5 tablespoons olive oil
1 × 15 ml spoon/1 tablespoon lemon juice	1 tablespoon lemon juice
1 × 15 ml spoon/1 tablespoon wine vinegar	1 tablespoon wine vinegar
1 clove garlic, crushed	1 clove garlic, crushed
salt	salt
freshly ground black pepper	freshly ground black pepper
1 × 2.5 ml spoon/1/2 teaspoon dried oregano	1/2 teaspoon dried oregano
To garnish:	To garnish:
2 × 15 ml spoons/2 tablespoons chopped parsley	2 tablespoons chopped parsley
2 × 15 ml spoons/2 tablespoons grated Parmesan cheese	2 tablespoons grated Parmesan cheese
4 lemon twists	4 lemon twists

First, make the dressing: mix together the oil, lemon juice, vinegar, garlic and salt and pepper to taste. Add the oregano. Allow the dressing to stand for 1 hour for the flavours to blend.

Cook the macaroni in a large pan of boiling salted water for 10 minutes until tender but al dente. Drain thoroughly.

Meanwhile, melt the butter in a small pan, add the mushrooms and sauté for 3 minutes. Drain on kitchen paper towels. While still warm, mix the pasta with the mussels, prawns (shrimp) and anchovies. Add the mushrooms and tomatoes and pour over the dressing. Mix thoroughly and turn into a serving dish. Chill in the refrigerator for 2 hours.

Sprinkle over the chopped parsley and Parmesan cheese and garnish with lemon twists. Serve immediately.
SERVES 4 TO 6

Sardinian Seafood Salad

LINGUINE WITH ANCHOVY AND COURGETTE SAUCE

METRIC/IMPERIAL	AMERICAN
450 g/1 lb linguine*	1 lb linguine*
150 g/5 oz butter	½ cup and two tablespoons butter
3 × 15 ml spoons/3 tablespoons olive oil	3 tablespoons olive oil
6 firm young courgettes, thinly sliced	6 firm young zucchini, thinly sliced
6 flat anchovy fillets, finely chopped	6 flat anchovy fillets, finely chopped
3 large, ripe tomatoes, peeled, seeded and chopped	3 large, ripe tomatoes, skinned, seeded and chopped
salt	salt
freshly ground black pepper	freshly ground black pepper
20 g/⅔ oz finely chopped parsley	½ cup finely chopped parsley
50 g/2 oz freshly grated Parmesan cheese	½ cup freshly grated Parmesan cheese

Cook the linguine in plenty of boiling, salted water until tender but *al dente*.

Meanwhile put 75 g/3 oz (6 tablespoons) of the butter and the oil into a large, heavy frying pan (skillet) over a medium heat. When butter and oil have melted add the courgettes (zucchini) and stir and cook until tender, about 3 minutes. Add the anchovies and tomatoes and cook a further few minutes until tomatoes are softened. Taste and season with salt and pepper – be careful with the salt, as the anchovies are salty.

Drain the linguine and place in a heated serving bowl. Add the remaining butter cut into small pieces, the parsley, and grated cheese, and toss to combine. Pour the sauce over and toss lightly again. Serve immediately on heated plates.

*Note Linguine are narrow, flat ribbons of pasta. If unavailable, use tagliatelle or other flat noodles.

SERVES 6

SMOKED HADDOCK AND EGG LASAGNE

METRIC/IMPERIAL	AMERICAN
450 ml/¾ pint white sauce	2 cups white sauce
100 g/4 oz Cheddar cheese, grated	1 cup grated Cheddar cheese
175 g/6 oz cooked smoked haddock fillet, skinned, boned and flaked	6 oz cooked smoked haddock fillet, skinned, boned and flaked
4 × 15 ml spoons/4 tablespoons single cream	4 tablespoons light cream
salt	salt
freshly ground black pepper	freshly ground black pepper
175 g/6 oz pre-cooked lasagne verde	6 oz pre-cooked lasagne verde
3 eggs	3 eggs
25 g/1 oz butter	2 tablespoons butter

Heat the sauce in a pan with half the grated cheese, haddock, cream, salt and pepper. Butter a shallow oven-proof dish. Spread a layer of fish sauce over the bottom and cover with an overlapping layer of lasagne. Repeat layers, finishing with a layer of sauce. Place in a moderately hot oven (190°C/375°F, Gas Mark 5) and bake for 30 minutes.

Meanwhile, beat the eggs with salt and pepper to taste. Melt the butter in a frying pan (skillet) and add the eggs. Cook, stirring, over a gentle heat until the eggs begin to scramble. Remove from the heat and immediately spoon over the lasagne. Sprinkle with the remaining cheese and return to the oven for 10 minutes. Serve immediately.

SERVES 4 TO 6

RED MULLET (SNAPPER) CALABRESE

METRIC/IMPERIAL	AMERICAN
4 red mullet, each weighing about 225 g/8 oz	2 red snapper, each weighing about 1 lb
salt	salt
2 × 15 ml spoons/2 tablespoons olive oil	2 tablespoons olive oil
1 × 15 ml spoon/1 tablespoon chopped fresh marjoram or 1 × 5 ml spoon/1 teaspoon dried marjoram	1 tablespoon chopped fresh marjoram or 1 teaspoon dried marjoram
40 g/1½ oz butter	3 tablespoons butter
2 × 15 ml spoons/2 tablespoons capers	2 tablespoons capers
12 black olives, stoned and slivered	12 ripe olives, pitted and slivered
thinly pared rind of ½ lemon	thinly pared zest of ½ lemon
1 × 15 ml spoon/1 tablespoon chopped parsley	1 tablespoon chopped parsley

Clean and gut the fish. Sprinkle the insides with salt. Heat the oil and marjoram in a large heavy based frying pan (skillet), and sauté the mullet (snapper) over moderate heat for 6 to 8 minutes each side, turning once.

Meanwhile, melt the butter in a small saucepan until it begins to turn brown, then remove from the heat and stir in the capers, olives, lemon rind (zest) and parsley. Carefully transfer the cooked fish to a warm serving plate and pour the hot sauce over the fish. Serve immediately.

SERVES 4

MULLET (SNAPPER) IN A PARCEL

METRIC/IMPERIAL	AMERICAN
2 × 15 ml spoons/2 tablespoons olive oil	2 tablespoons olive oil
2 cloves garlic, crushed	2 cloves garlic, crushed
1 × 2.5 ml spoon/½ teaspoon dried fennel	½ teaspoon dried fennel
1 red pepper, seeded and sliced	1 red pepper, seeded and sliced
1 green pepper, seeded and sliced	1 green pepper, seeded and sliced
2 onions, sliced	2 onions, sliced
450 g/1 lb courgettes, sliced	1 lb zucchini, sliced
225 g/8 oz mushrooms, sliced	2 cups sliced mushrooms
4 red mullet	2 red snapper
salt	salt
freshly ground black pepper	freshly ground black pepper

Heat the oil in a large frying pan (skillet). Gently sauté the garlic, fennel, peppers, onions, courgettes (zucchini) and mushrooms for 7 minutes until tender.

Meanwhile, clean and gut the fish and leave whole. Place each fish on a piece of foil and season with salt and pepper. Place the vegetables around each fish and fold over the foil to make individual parcels. Place in a preheated moderately hot oven (190°C/375°F, Gas Mark 5) and cook for 30 (45) minutes. Serve immediately.

SERVES 4

MEDITERRANEAN MULLET (SNAPPER)

METRIC/IMPERIAL	AMERICAN
4 red mullet	2 red snapper
25 g/1 oz butter plus extra for greasing	2 tablespoons butter, plus extra for greasing
2 tomatoes, peeled and sliced	2 tomatoes, skinned and sliced
1 green pepper, seeded and sliced	1 green pepper, seeded and sliced
100 g/4 oz mushrooms, sliced	1 cup sliced mushrooms
salt	salt
freshly ground black pepper	freshly ground black pepper
4 × 15 ml spoons/4 tablespoons red wine	4 tablespoons red wine
chopped chives to garnish	chopped chives to garnish

Clean and gut the fish and leave whole. Grease a large shallow casserole. Melt the butter in a frying pan (skillet) and sauté the tomatoes, pepper and mushrooms for 5 minutes until soft. Season with salt and pepper.

Lay the fish in the casserole and spoon over the vegetables. Pour in the wine, season with more salt and pepper and cover. Place in a preheated moderately hot oven (190°C/375°F, Gas Mark 5) and cook for 30 (45) minutes. Sprinkle with chives and serve immediately, straight from the casserole.

SERVES 4

Mediterranean Mullet

ITALIAN FISH STEW

METRIC/IMPERIAL	AMERICAN
300 ml/½ pint mussels	1¼ cups mussels
5 × 15 ml spoons/5 tablespoons olive oil	5 tablespoons olive oil
1 onion, sliced	1 onion, sliced
1 clove garlic, crushed	1 clove garlic, crushed
225 g/8 oz carrots, peeled and cut into strips	½ lb carrots, peeled and cut into strips
1 × 397 g/14 oz can tomatoes	1 × 16 oz can tomatoes
100 g/4 oz black olives	¾ cup ripe olives
1 bay leaf	1 bay leaf
salt	salt
freshly ground black pepper	freshly ground black pepper
4 slices white bread	4 slices white bread
750 g/1½ lb white fish	1½ lb white fish
2 × 15 ml spoons/2 tablespoons chopped parsley	2 tablespoons chopped parsley

First, prepare the mussels: cover with cold water, discarding any which are open or float to the top. Scrub the mussels to remove any barnacles and remove the beards. Soak in fresh cold water until ready to cook. Drain.

Melt 2 × 15 ml spoons/2 tablespoons oil in a frying pan (skillet) and sauté the onion, garlic and carrots for 5 minutes until soft. Add the tomatoes with their juice, olives, bay leaf and season with salt and pepper. Simmer for 15 minutes.

Meanwhile cut four circles from the slices of bread and sauté in the remaining oil until crisp and golden. Drain on kitchen paper towels and keep warm.

Add the fish to the stew and cook for 5 minutes. Add the mussels and cook for another 10 minutes or until the shells open. Discard any mussels which do not open. Adjust the seasoning and remove the bay leaf.

Put a croûte of fried bread in the bottom of 4 large warm soup bowls. Place the white fish on top. Gently pour over the vegetables and mussels. Sprinkle with parsley and serve immediately.

SERVES 4

FRESH TUNA WITH TOMATOES

METRIC/IMPERIAL	AMERICAN
4 tuna steaks	4 tuna steaks,
salt	salt
freshly ground black pepper	freshly ground black pepper
flour for dusting	flour for dusting
3 × 15 ml spoons/3 tablespoons olive oil	3 tablespoons olive oil
1 small onion, chopped	1 small onion, chopped
1 clove garlic, crushed	1 clove garlic, crushed
750 g/1½ lb tomatoes, peeled and chopped	1½ lb tomatoes, skinned and chopped
2 × 15 ml spoons/2 tablespoons chopped parsley	2 tablespoons chopped parsley
1 bay leaf	1 bay leaf
4 anchovy fillets, mashed	4 anchovy fillets, mashed
6 black olives	6 ripe olives

Season the fish with salt and pepper and dust with flour. Heat half the oil in a large shallow frying pan (skillet). Sauté the fish quickly until golden on both sides. Carefully transfer to a plate.

Add the remaining oil to the pan, add the onion and garlic and sauté for 5 minutes until soft. Add the tomatoes, parsley, bay leaf and anchovies and stir for a few seconds. Bring to the boil and continue boiling until the mixture has reduced to a thin sauce. Season with pepper, return the fish to the pan and simmer gently for 15 minutes, turning once. Turn off the heat, add the olives and leave for 5 minutes. Transfer to a warm serving dish and serve immediately.
SERVES 4

FRITTO MISTO DI MARE

METRIC/IMPERIAL	AMERICAN
100 g/4 oz plain flour	1 cup all-purpose flour
salt	salt
2 × 15 ml spoons/2 tablespoons olive oil	2 tablespoons olive oil
150 ml/¼ pint tepid water	⅔ cup tepid water
1 egg white	1 egg white
oil for deep frying	oil for deep frying
1 kg/2 lb mixed fish, cut into small pieces	2 lb mixed fish, cut into small pieces
lemon wedges	lemon wedges
sprigs of parsley	sprigs of parsley

To make the batter: sieve the flour and salt into a bowl and make a well in the centre. Pour in the oil and gradually beat in the water to form a smooth, thick batter. Refrigerate for about 2 hours. Immediately before using, whisk the egg white stiffly and fold lightly into the batter.

Heat the oil in a deep fryer to 190°C/375°F. Line a baking tin (pan) with crumpled kitchen paper. Coat fish in the batter. Cook each type of fish separately for 3 to 6 minutes, depending on size. Lift out, drain on the crumpled paper and keep hot in a preheated moderate oven (180°C/350°F, Gas Mark 4) until all the fish are fried. Allow the fat to regain frying temperature before cooking each batch.

Pile the fish on a warm serving dish and garnish with lemon wedges and sprigs of parsley. Serve immediately.
SERVES 4

TUNA FISH SALAD

METRIC/IMPERIAL	AMERICAN
2 × 200 g/7 oz cans tuna	2 × 7 oz cans tuna
freshly ground black pepper	freshly ground black pepper
4 × 5 ml spoons/4 teaspoons capers	4 teaspoons capers
4 tomatoes, thinly sliced	4 tomatoes, thinly sliced
1 onion, finely sliced	1 onion, finely sliced
2 × 5 ml spoons/2 teaspoons lemon juice	2 teaspoons lemon juice

Drain the tuna, reserving 1 × 15 ml spoon/1 tablespoon of the oil. Flake the fish with a fork and arrange in piles in the centre of 6 shallow individual serving dishes.

Sprinkle with black pepper and the capers. Surround with slices of tomato topped with onion. Add the lemon juice to the reserved oil and sprinkle a little over each portion. Serve immediately.
SERVES 6

TROUT WITH MUSHROOMS

METRIC/IMPERIAL	AMERICAN
4 trout, each about 275 g/10 oz	4 trout, each about 10 oz
salt	salt
freshly ground black pepper	freshly ground black pepper
flour for coating	flour for coating
1 × 15 ml spoon/1 tablespoon oil	1 tablespoon oil
75 g/3 oz butter	6 tablespoons butter
2 spring onions, finely sliced	2 scallions, finely sliced
350 g/12 oz mushrooms, sliced	3 cups sliced mushrooms
1 × 15 ml spoon/1 tablespoon chopped parsley	1 tablespoon chopped parsley
juice of ½ lemon	juice of ½ lemon
25 g/1 oz dry white breadcrumbs	½ cup dry white bread crumbs
To garnish:	To garnish:
lemon quarters	lemon quarters
sprigs of parsley	sprigs of parsley

Wash the trout, leaving the heads and tails on, and pat dry with kitchen paper towels. Season inside and out with salt and pepper and coat lightly with flour. Heat the oil and 25 g/1 oz (2 tablespoons) of the butter in a large frying pan (skillet) and sauté the trout gently for 6 to 8 minutes on each side, until lightly browned.

In another pan, melt 40 g/1½ oz (3 tablespoons) butter and sauté the spring onions (scallions) and mushrooms for 5 minutes until soft. Add salt, parsley and lemon juice, and toss lightly.

Arrange the trout side by side on a large warm serving dish with rows of mushrooms in between them. Keep hot. Quickly sauté the breadcrumbs in the pan in which the fish were cooked, add more butter if necessary, until crisp. Sprinkle over the fish and garnish with lemon and parsley. Serve immediately.
SERVES 4

Fresh Tuna with Tomatoes

MUSSELS ITALIAN STYLE

METRIC/IMPERIAL	AMERICAN
2.25 litres/4 pints mussels	10 cups mussels
bouquet garni	bouquet garni
100 ml/4 fl oz water	1/2 cup water
100 ml/4 fl oz dry white wine	1/2 cup dry white wine
salt	salt
freshly ground black pepper	freshly ground black pepper
2 × 15 ml spoons/2 tablespoons finely chopped shallot	2 tablespoons finely chopped shallot
1 clove garlic, crushed	1 clove garlic, crushed
2 × 15 ml spoons/2 tablespoons finely chopped parsley	2 tablespoons finely chopped parsley
75 g/3 oz fresh breadcrumbs	1½ cups fresh bread crumbs
3 × 15 ml spoons/3 tablespoons grated Parmesan cheese	3 tablespoons grated Parmesan cheese
25 g/1 oz butter	2 tablespoons butter

First, prepare the mussels; cover with cold water, discarding any which are open or float to the top. Scrub the mussels to remove any barnacles, and remove the beards. Soak in fresh cold water until ready to cook. Drain.

Place the mussels in a deep saucepan, add the bouquet garni, salt and pepper and pour over the water and wine.

Cover the pan and cook over moderate heat until the mussels open, shaking the pan occasionally. Discard any mussels that do not open. Strain and reserve the liquid. Remove the empty half of each shell, then place the remaining shells, mussel side up, close together in a large shallow casserole. Sprinkle with the shallot, garlic, parsley, breadcrumbs and cheese. Dot with butter.

Reduce the fish liquid to half by boiling rapidly in a small saucepan. Pour sauce round, not over, the dish. Place in a preheated moderate oven (180°C/350°F, Gas Mark 4) and bake for 15 minutes. Serve immediately.
SERVES 4

MUSSELS IN TOMATO SAUCE

METRIC/IMPERIAL	AMERICAN
2.25 litres/4 pints mussels	10 cups mussels
4 × 15 ml spoons/4 tablespoons olive oil	4 tablespoons olive oil
2 garlic cloves, peeled and crushed	2 garlic cloves, peeled and crushed
7 × 15 ml spoons/7 tablespoons dry white wine	7 tablespoons dry white wine
2 × 15 ml spoons/2 tablespoons tomato puree	2 tablespoons tomato paste
4 × 15 ml spoons/4 tablespoons water	4 tablespoons water
salt	salt
freshly ground black pepper	freshly ground black pepper
25 g/1 oz butter	2 tablespoons butter
25 g/1 oz plain flour	1/4 cup all-purpose flour
250 ml/8 fl oz milk	1 cup milk
2 × 15 ml spoons/2 tablespoons grated Parmesan cheese	2 tablespoons grated Parmesan cheese

First, prepare the mussels; cover with cold water, discarding any which are open or float to the top. Scrub the mussels to remove any barnacles and remove the beards. Soak in fresh cold water until ready to cook. Drain.

Put the mussels in a pan with half the oil. Cook over high heat for 5 minutes or until the mussels open, discarding any that do not. Strain the cooking liquid and reserve. Remove the mussels from their shells.

Heat the remaining oil in a pan, add the garlic and fry gently until golden brown. Add the wine and cooking liquid. Simmer for 5 minutes, then add the tomato puree (paste) diluted with the water. Season with salt and pepper to taste and simmer for 5 minutes.

Meanwhile, melt the butter in a small pan, add the flour and cook, stirring, for 1 minute. Stir in the milk gradually and cook, stirring, over low heat until the sauce thickens.

Stir the mussels into the tomato mixture and spoon into a shallow ovenproof dish. Pour over the sauce and sprinkle with the cheese. Bake in a preheated moderately hot oven (190°C/375°F, Gas Mark 5) for 15 minutes. Serve hot.
SERVES 4

NEAPOLITAN SCAMPI

METRIC/IMPERIAL	AMERICAN
50 g/2 oz plain flour	½ cup all-purpose flour
salt	salt
freshly ground black pepper	freshly ground black pepper
450 g/1 lb scampi	1 lb jumbo shrimp
25 g/1 oz butter	2 tablespoons butter
100 g/4 oz mushrooms, sliced	1 cup sliced mushrooms
225 g/8 oz tomatoes, peeled, seeded and diced	½ lb tomatoes, skinned, seeded and diced
150 ml/¼ pint double cream	½ cup heavy cream
chopped parsley to garnish	chopped parsley to garnish
Sauce:	Sauce:
150 ml/¼ pint dry white wine	½ cup dry white wine
1 small onion, finely chopped	1 small onion, finely chopped
1 bouquet garni	1 bouquet garni
25 g/1 oz butter	2 tablespoons butter
25 g/1 oz plain flour	¼ cup all-purpose flour
1 clove garlic, crushed	1 clove garlic, crushed
2 × 5 ml spoons/2 teaspoons tomato purée	2 teaspoons tomato paste
300 ml/½ pint chicken stock	1¼ cups chicken bouillon
salt	salt
freshly ground black pepper	freshly ground black pepper

First, make the sauce: pour the wine into a small saucepan, add the onion and bouquet garni, bring to the boil, then reduce to half by boiling rapidly. Set aside.

Melt the butter in another small saucepan. Remove from the heat and stir in the flour. Return the pan to the heat and cook for 2 minutes. Remove from the heat, then stir in the garlic, tomato purée (paste), stock (bouillon) and salt and pepper to taste. Bring to the boil then simmer for 15 minutes. Remove the bouquet garni from the wine mixture then stir into the sauce mixture. Simmer for a further 10 minutes. Set aside.

Season the flour with salt and pepper. Coat the fish in the flour, shaking off any excess. Melt the butter in a frying pan (skillet) and sauté the fish gently for about 5 minutes. Remove to a warm serving dish. Add the mushrooms to the pan and cook for 2 minutes. Stir in the sauce, tomatoes and cream, taste and adjust seasoning, bring to the boil and pour over the fish. Garnish with the parsley and serve very hot with buttered noodles.

SERVES 4

Neapolitan Scampi

MEAT

BEEF BRAISED IN RED WINE

METRIC/IMPERIAL	AMERICAN
1.5 kg/3 lb joint of topside, chuck or rolled brisket	3 lb top round, chuck roast or rolled brisket
2 onions, 1 sliced, 1 chopped very finely	2 onions, 1 sliced, 1 chopped very finely
1 carrot, sliced	1 carrot, sliced
1 celery stick, sliced	1 celery stalk, sliced
2 cloves garlic, crushed	2 cloves garlic, crushed
2 bay leaves	2 bay leaves
6 peppercorns	6 peppercorns
225 ml/8 fl oz red wine	1 cup red wine
25 g/1 oz bacon fat or dripping	2 tablespoons fatback or drippings
salt	salt
freshly ground black pepper	freshly ground black pepper

Put the meat into a deep bowl. Add the sliced onion, carrot, celery, garlic, bay leaves, peppercorns and wine to the meat. Cover and place in the refrigerator to marinate for 24 hours, turning several times.

Lift the meat out of the marinade and dry it carefully. Heat the fat in a flameproof casserole into which the meat will fit fairly closely. Sauté the chopped onion for 5 minutes until soft. Put in the meat, increase the heat and brown the meat on all sides. Pour in the strained marinade and bring to the boil. Season with salt and pepper, lower the heat, cover tightly and simmer very gently for at least 3 hours or until the meat is tender, turning the meat once half-way through. Transfer meat to a carving dish.

At the end of the cooking there should be just enough sauce to moisten each portion. If there is too much, reduce the sauce by rapid boiling; if too little, add a little water.

Slice the meat fairly thickly and arrange on a warm serving dish. Skim any surface fat from the sauce, adjust the seasoning and spoon over the meat. Serve immediately.

SERVES 6

BEEF OLIVES WITH ARTICHOKES

METRIC/IMPERIAL	AMERICAN
2 young globe artichokes	2 young globe artichokes
salt	salt
juice of 1 lemon	juice of 1 lemon
8 slices beef topside, each weighing 50 g/2 oz	8 slices beef top round, each weighing 2 oz
100 g/4 oz Prosciutto or raw smoked ham finely chopped	1/4 lb Prosciutto or raw smoked ham, finely chopped
50 g/2 oz butter	1/4 cup butter
2 × 15 ml spoons/2 tablespoons olive oil	2 tablespoons olive oil
1 small onion, peeled and chopped	1 small onion, peeled and chopped
flour for coating	flour for coating
4–5 × 15 ml spoons/4–5 tablespoons dry white wine	4–5 tablespoons dry white wine
freshly ground black pepper	freshly ground black pepper
6–8 × 15 ml spoons 6–8 tablespoons hot beef stock	6–8 tablespoons hot beef stock

Discard the outer leaves, tips and chokes from the artichokes. Cook them in plenty of boiling salted water, with the lemon juice added, for 20 minutes. Drain and cut each one into 8 sections.

Beat the meat slices with a mallet to flatten. Mix the ham with a third of the butter and spread this mixture over the slices. Top each one with 2 artichoke sections, then roll the slices around the stuffing and tie securely with string.

Heat the remaining butter and the oil in a flameproof casserole, add the onion and fry gently for 5 minutes. Coat the meat rolls with flour, add to the casserole and fry, turning, until browned on all sides.

Add the wine and salt and pepper to taste. Lower the heat, cover the casserole and cook gently for about 45 minutes or until the meat is tender. Turn the meat during cooking and add the stock as necessary to prevent the meat sticking.

Remove the meat from the casserole and untie the string. Arrange the meat on a warmed serving platter, then pour over the cooking juices. Serve immediately.

SERVES 4

STEAK WITH FRESH TOMATO SAUCE

METRIC/IMPERIAL
4 rib or rump steaks, 2 cm/¾ inch thick
salt
freshly ground black pepper
olive oil
Sauce:
2 × 15 ml spoons/2 tablespoons olive oil
3 cloves garlic, crushed
450 g/1 lb tomatoes, peeled, seeded and chopped
few fresh basil leaves, chopped, or 1 × 2.5 ml spoon/½ teaspoon dried oregano
parsley sprigs to garnish (optional)

AMERICAN
4 rib or rump steaks, ¾ inch thick
salt
freshly ground black pepper
olive oil
Sauce:
2 tablespoons olive oil
3 cloves garlic, crushed
2 cups skinned, seeded and chopped tomatoes
few fresh basil leaves, chopped, or ½ teaspoon dried oregano
parsley sprigs to garnish (optional)

Beat the steaks with a rolling pin or mallet to tenderize. Season with salt and pepper. Sprinkle with oil and leave to stand.

To make the sauce: heat the oil in a saucepan and sauté the garlic for 1 minute. Add the tomatoes with salt and pepper to taste. Bring to the boil then cook over moderate heat for 5 minutes, until the tomatoes are just softened. Add basil or oregano.

Oil the base of a large frying pan (skillet) and sauté the steaks over moderate heat for 2 minutes on each side, until lightly browned. Top each steak with a thick layer of the sauce, cover the pan tightly and cook over a low heat for 6 to 10 minutes or until the steaks are tender and cooked to your liking. Transfer the steaks to a warm serving plate, garnish with the parsley if using, and serve immediately.
SERVES 4

Lamb Kebabs Roma

BEEF STEAKS WITH LEMON

METRIC/IMPERIAL	AMERICAN
4 thin rump steaks	4 thin top round steaks
4 × 15 ml spoons/4 tablespoons white wine	4 tablespoons white wine
2 × 15 ml spoons/2 tablespoons olive oil	2 tablespoons olive oil
juice of 1 lemon	juice of 1 lemon
salt	salt
freshly ground black pepper	freshly ground black pepper
1 clove garlic, crushed	1 clove garlic, crushed
1 × 2.5 ml spoon/½ teaspoon dried oregano	½ teaspoon dried oregano
lemon quarters to garnish	lemon quarters to garnish

Beat the steaks with a rolling pin or mallet to tenderize. Place in a large shallow glass bowl. Mix all the other ingredients together except the lemon quarters and pour over the meat in the bowl. Leave to marinate in a cool place for 2 hours.

Drain off the marinade. Grill (broil) the steaks under a preheated hot grill (broiler) for 5 minutes on each side. Arrange on a warm serving plate, garnish with lemon quarters and serve immediately.

SERVES 4

LAMB KEBABS ROMA

METRIC/IMPERIAL	AMERICAN
½ shoulder lamb, boned and cubed	1 lb boneless lamb, cubed
1 small green pepper, seeded and cut into 8 pieces	1 small green pepper, seeded and cut into 8 pieces
2 lambs' kidneys, skinned, cored and halved	2 lamb kidneys, skinned, cored and halved
2 onions, quartered	2 onions, quartered
4 tomatoes, halved	4 tomatoes, halved
4 mushrooms, halved	4 mushrooms, halved
Marinade:	Marinade:
2 × 15 ml spoons/2 tablespoons olive oil	2 tablespoons olive oil
2 × 15 ml spoons/2 tablespoons wine vinegar	2 tablespoons wine vinegar
pinch of mixed dried herbs	pinch of mixed dried herbs
pinch of sugar	pinch of sugar
pinch of dry mustard	pinch of dry mustard
1 clove garlic, crushed	1 clove garlic, crushed
salt	salt
freshly ground black pepper	freshly ground black pepper

Put the lamb cubes into a glass bowl. Mix the marinade ingredients together and pour over the lamb. Leave for 3 hours in a cool place, turning occasionally.

Thread the lamb, green pepper, kidneys, onion, tomatoes and mushrooms onto 4 skewers and baste with the marinade. Place under a preheated hot grill (broiler) and grill (broil), turning frequently, until cooked. Transfer to a warm serving plate and serve immediately.

SERVES 4

TUSCANY LAMB CASSEROLE

METRIC/IMPERIAL	AMERICAN
1 best end neck of lamb	1 lamb rib rack
4 × 15 ml spoons/4 tablespoons olive oil	¼ cup olive oil
1 bay leaf	1 bay leaf
salt	salt
freshly ground black pepper	freshly ground black pepper
150 ml/¼ pint white wine	⅔ cup white wine
1 red pepper, seeded and sliced	1 red pepper, seeded and sliced
1 clove garlic, crushed	1 clove garlic, crushed
1 × 15 ml spoon/1 tablespoon chopped parsley	1 tablespoon chopped parsley

Place the lamb in a casserole with half the oil and bay leaf and season with salt and pepper. Cover, place in a preheated moderately hot oven (190°C/375°F, Gas Mark 5) and cook, allowing 25 minutes per 450 g/1 lb. Baste and turn the meat occasionally. When it begins to brown, add the wine and continue to baste occasionally.

Ten minutes before the end of the cooking time, heat the remaining oil in a small saucepan. Sauté the red pepper, garlic and parsley together for 5 minutes. Pour all the juices from the casserole over the pepper mixture, removing the bay leaf. Transfer the lamb to a warm serving plate and divide into cutlets. Spoon the sauce over and serve immediately.

SERVES 4

LAMB CHOPS WITH ROSEMARY

METRIC/IMPERIAL	AMERICAN
50 g/2 oz butter, softened	¼ cup softened butter
4 lamb chops	4 lamb chops
chopped fresh rosemary	chopped fresh rosemary
freshly ground black pepper	freshly ground black pepper

Spread a little of the butter on each of the lamb chops. Sprinkle with rosemary and black pepper. Place the chops under a preheated hot grill (broiler) and grill (broil) for 7 minutes on each side until cooked.

Transfer the lamb chops to a warm serving plate and serve immediately.

SERVES 4

LAMB IN EGG AND LEMON SAUCE

METRIC/IMPERIAL	AMERICAN
25 g/1 oz lard	2 tablespoons shortening
3 lean bacon rashers, diced	3 lean bacon slices, diced
1 small onion, chopped	1 small onion, chopped
750 g/1½ lb shoulder of lamb, boned and cubed	1½ lb boneless lamb, cubed
2 × 15 ml spoons/2 tablespoons plain flour	2 tablespoons all-purpose flour
salt	salt
freshly ground black pepper	freshly ground black pepper
4 × 15 ml spoons/4 tablespoons white wine	¼ cup white wine
450 ml/¾ pint stock or water	2 cups bouillon or water
2 egg yolks	2 egg yolks
juice of ½ lemon	juice of ½ lemon
1 × 15 ml spoon/1 tablespoon chopped parsley	1 tablespoon chopped parsley
1 × 5 ml spoon/1 teaspoon chopped fresh marjoram or ½ × 2.5 ml spoon/¼ teaspoon dried marjoram	1 teaspoon chopped fresh marjoram or ¼ teaspoon dried marjoram

Melt the fat in a saucepan and sauté the bacon for 2 minutes until the fat begins to run. Add the onion and lamb and sauté, stirring frequently, until golden.

Sprinkle in the flour with salt and pepper to taste and cook, stirring, for 1 to 2 minutes. Add the wine and allow to bubble until almost completely evaporated, then stir in the stock (bouillon) or water and bring to the boil.

Cover tightly and simmer very gently for 45 minutes or until the meat is tender, stirring occasionally. Skim off any fat that may have risen to the surface.

Just before serving, beat together the egg yolks, lemon juice, parsley and marjoram and stir in 3 × 15 ml spoons/3 tablespoons of the hot lamb stock. Stir into the lamb mixture and cook over low heat, stirring constantly, until the egg has cooked and the sauce is thick enough to coat the back of a wooden spoon. Do not allow to boil or the sauce will curdle. Adjust the seasoning, transfer to a warmed serving dish and serve immediately.
SERVES 4

TUSCAN ROAST LAMB

METRIC/IMPERIAL	AMERICAN
1 × 1 kg/2 lb leg of lamb	2 lb leg of lamb
100 g/4 oz bacon, chopped	½ cup chopped bacon
3 garlic cloves, chopped	3 garlic cloves, chopped
2 sprigs rosemary	4 tablespoons olive oil
4 × 15 ml spoons/4 tablespoons olive oil	salt
salt	freshly ground black pepper
freshly ground black pepper	

Make incisions in the meat and insert bacon, garlic and the rosemary. With half the oil, grease a roasting pan and place the lamb in it. Sprinkle with salt and pepper and the remaining oil. Roast in a preheated moderately hot oven (190°C/375°F, Gas Mark 5) for 1½ hours or until the meat is tender, basting occasionally. Transfer to a warmed platter and serve immediately.
SERVES 4

LAMB WITH SWEET PEPPERS

METRIC/IMPERIAL	AMERICAN
1 kg/2 lb neck lamb cutlets	2 lb lamb rib chops
salt	salt
freshly ground black pepper	freshly ground black pepper
flour	flour
2 × 15 ml spoons/2 tablespoons olive oil	2 tablespoons olive oil
2 cloves garlic, crushed	2 cloves garlic, crushed
300 ml/½ pint dry white wine	1¼ cups dry white wine
3 red peppers, seeded and quartered	3 red peppers, seeded and quartered
3 green peppers, seeded and quartered	3 green peppers, seeded and quartered
4 tomatoes, peeled and quartered	4 tomatoes, skinned and quartered
1 bay leaf	1 bay leaf

Trim excess fat from the meat, season with salt and pepper, and coat with flour.

Heat the olive oil in a large flameproof casserole, and sauté the garlic for 1 minute. Add the meat and sauté until lightly browned, turning once or twice. Pour in the wine and allow to bubble briskly for a few minutes until reduced by one-third.

Add the peppers, tomatoes and bay leaf to the lamb. Cover tightly and simmer very gently for 45 minutes or until the lamb is tender. Adjust the seasoning and serve immediately, from the casserole.

SERVES 4

PORK ON A SKEWER

METRIC/IMPERIAL	AMERICAN
450 g/1 lb pork fillet	1 lb pork tenderloin
2–3 slices firm bread, 1 cm/½ inch thick	2–3 slices firm bread, ½ inch thick
100 g/4 oz thinly sliced proscuitto	¼ lb thinly sliced proscuitto
8 bay leaves, halved	8 bay leaves, halved
olive oil	olive oil
salt	salt
freshly ground black pepper	freshly ground black pepper

Cut the pork into 12 cubes. Remove the crusts and cut the bread into 12 cubes of about the same size as the meat. Remove any rind and cut the proscuitto into 12 pieces. Thread the pork, proscuitto, bay leaves and bread alternately on 4 kebab skewers. Lay the skewers flat, slightly apart, in a well oiled baking tin (pan). Sprinkle with salt and pepper, and then liberally with oil.

Place in the centre of a preheated moderately hot oven (190°C/375°F, Gas Mark 5) and cook for 30 to 40 minutes until the meat is tender and the bread crisp and crunchy. Turn the skewers once half-way through cooking. Transfer to a warm serving plate and serve immediately.

SERVES 4

Lamb in Egg and Lemon Sauce; Lamb with Sweet Peppers; Pork on a Skewer

PORK CHOPS IN WINE

METRIC/IMPERIAL
4 thick pork chops, trimmed of
  excess fat
salt
freshly ground black pepper
2 × 15 ml spoons/2
  tablespoons olive oil
2 cloves garlic, crushed
2 × 15 ml spoons/2
  tablespoons chopped parsley
200 ml/⅓ pint light dry red
  wine

AMERICAN
4 center cut pork chops,
  trimmed of excess fat
salt
freshly ground black pepper
2 tablespoons olive oil
2 cloves garlic, crushed
2 tablespoons chopped parsley
1 cup light dry red wine

Season the chops with salt and pepper. Heat the oil in a large frying pan (skillet) and sauté the chops, for 3 to 4 minutes on each side, until lightly browned. Transfer to a plate.

Add the garlic and parsley to the pan, stir and fry for 1 to 2 minutes, then pour in the wine and bring to simmering point. Return the chops to the pan, cover and simmer gently for 30 to 35 minutes, until tender.

Transfer the chops to a warm serving dish. Boil the pan juices rapidly, uncovered, until reduced by about half and spoon over the chops. Serve immediately.
SERVES 4

Pork Chops in Wine

PORK SLICES WITH YOGURT SAUCE

METRIC/IMPERIAL
750 g/1½ lb pork fillet, thinly
  sliced
2 × 15 ml spoons/2
  tablespoons plain flour,
  seasoned with salt and
  freshly ground black pepper
1 egg, beaten
50 g/2 oz fresh white
  breadcrumbs
4 × 15 ml spoons/4
  tablespoons olive oil
1 hard-boiled egg, roughly
  chopped
150 ml/¼ pint natural yogurt
1 lemon, sliced to garnish

AMERICAN
1½ lb pork tenderloin, thinly
  sliced
2 tablespoons all-purpose
  flour, seasoned with salt
  and freshly ground black
  pepper
1 egg, beaten
1 cup soft white bread crumbs
4 tablespoons olive oil
1 hard-cooked egg, roughly
  chopped
⅔ cup unflavoured yogurt
1 lemon, sliced to garnish

Coat the pork with the seasoned flour. Dip the pork in the beaten egg and then coat with breadcrumbs.

Heat the oil in a frying pan (skillet) and sauté the pork slices until golden brown. Drain, arrange on a warm serving dish and keep hot. Mix together the egg and yogurt. Heat through gently and pour over the pork. Garnish with the slices of lemon and serve immediately.
SERVES 4

NEAPOLITAN PORK CHOPS

METRIC/IMPERIAL	AMERICAN
2 × 15 ml spoons/2 tablespoons olive oil	2 tablespoons olive oil
1 clove garlic, crushed	1 clove garlic, crushed
4 thick pork chops	4 center cut pork chops
salt	salt
freshly ground black pepper	freshly ground black pepper
3 × 15 ml spoons/3 tablespoons white wine	3 tablespoons white wine
3 × 15 ml spoons/3 tablespoons tomato purée	3 tablespoons tomato paste
1 green pepper, seeded and chopped	1 green pepper, seeded and chopped
350 g/12 oz mushrooms, sliced	3 cups sliced mushrooms

Heat the oil in a large frying pan (skillet) and sauté the garlic until brown. Discard the garlic. Add the chops and sauté on both sides until brown. Sprinkle with salt and pepper.

Mix the wine and tomato purée (paste) together and add to the pan. Add the green pepper and mushrooms and cook, covered, over low heat for 45 minutes or until the chops are cooked. Transfer to a warm serving plate and serve immediately.

SERVES 4

PORK COOKED IN MILK

METRIC/IMPERIAL	AMERICAN
1 kg/2 lb boneless leg or loin of pork, derinded	2 lb boneless leg or pork loin blade roast, derinded
salt	salt
freshly ground black pepper	freshly ground black pepper
1 clove garlic, crushed	1 clove garlic, crushed
4 coriander seeds, crushed	4 coriander seeds, crushed
40 g/1½ oz butter	3 tablespoons butter
1.2 litres/2 pints milk	5 cups milk

Season the inside of the meat with salt and pepper and sprinkle with the garlic and coriander. Roll up and tie securely with string. Melt the butter in a deep, heavy based saucepan into which the meat fits fairly closely. Brown the meat over gentle heat, turning to brown all over.

In another pan, bring the milk just to the boil. When the meat has browned, pour the milk over it; there should be just enough milk to cover. Simmer gently, uncovered, for about 1 hour.

Stir the skin that will have formed into the rest of the milk and continue cooking for 30 to 45 minutes, until the meat is tender and the milk reduced to about 250 ml/⅓ pint (1 cup). Lift out the meat, slice, and arrange in a warm shallow serving dish. Keep hot.

Beat the milk remaining in the pan lightly and scrape the juices from the bottom of the pan. It should be beige in colour, grainy in texture and creamy in consistency – if not, cook for a few more minutes, taking care that it does not burn. Spoon over the slices of pork and serve immediately, or cold

SERVES 6

POLENTA WITH SKEWERED MEATS

METRIC/IMPERIAL	AMERICAN
225 g/8 oz veal sweetbreads, soaked in cold water for 2 hours	½ lb veal sweetbreads, soaked in cold water for 2 hours
4 thick slices pickled belly pork	4 thick slices pickled salt pork
75 g/3 oz butter	6 tablespoons butter
6 chicken livers, halved	6 chicken livers, halved
225 g/8 oz slice of veal fillet	½ lb slice of veal fillet
16 small flat mushrooms	16 small flat mushrooms
8 fresh sage leaves	8 fresh sage leaves
salt	salt
freshly ground black pepper	freshly ground black pepper
4 lemon wedges to garnish	4 lemon wedges to garnish
Polenta:	Polenta:
750 ml/1¼ pints water	3 cups water
2 × 5 ml spoons/2 teaspoons salt	2 teaspoons salt
225 g/8 oz finely ground polenta	½ lb finely ground polenta
freshly ground black pepper	freshly ground black pepper

First, make the polenta: bring the water and salt to a steady boil in a saucepan. Slowly pour in the polenta, stirring all the time until smooth. Lower the heat and simmer, stirring frequently, for 25 to 30 minutes until thick. Season with pepper. Turn out onto a wooden board and shape into a circle about 2 cm/¾ inch thick. Leave to become cold. Cut into 4 triangular pieces.

Drain the sweetbreads, cover with fresh cold water, bring slowly to the boil and simmer for 15 minutes. Drain, immerse in cold water and peel away all skin and fat, then cut into 12 equal pieces.

Cut each slice of pork into 4 pieces. Place in a saucepan, cover with cold water and bring to the boil. Simmer for 15 minutes, then drain. Melt 25 g/1 oz (2 tablespoons) butter in a saucepan and sauté the chicken livers for about 2 minutes, turning to seal all sides, then drain. Beat out the veal until 5 mm/¼ inch thick, then cut into 3 cm/1¼ inch squares. Divide the meats into 4 equal portions

Thread the pieces of meat and mushrooms alternately onto 4 kebab skewers, starting and ending with pork and inserting a sage leaf occasionally. Season with salt and pepper. Melt 25 g/1 oz (2 tablespoons) butter in the pan in which the livers were fried and use to brush the kebabs. Place the kebabs under a preheated hot grill (broiler) and grill (broil) for about 10 minutes, turning several times and brushing with melted butter frequently to ensure the meat does not become dry.

Sauté the polenta slices gently in the remaining butter until golden brown on both sides. Arrange the polenta slices in a warm serving dish and lay the kebabs on top. Garnish with lemon wedges. Remove the meats from the skewers at the table and squeeze the lemon over them. Serve immediately.

SERVES 4

STUFFED MEAT ROLL

METRIC/IMPERIAL	AMERICAN
450 g/1 lb topside of beef, cut as one 1 cm/½ inch thick slice	1¼ lb top round of beef, cut as one ½ inch thick slice
salt	salt
freshly ground black pepper	freshly ground black pepper
50 g/2 oz crustless bread	2 oz crustless bread
milk for soaking	milk for soaking
225 g/8 oz minced shoulder of pork	1 cup ground shoulder of pork
225 g/8 oz minced lean beef	1 cup ground lean beef
2 eggs, lightly beaten	2 eggs, lightly beaten
40 g/1½ oz Parmesan or Pecorino cheese, finely grated	⅓ cup finely grated Parmesan or Pecorino cheese
1 × 15 ml spoon/1 tablespoon chopped parsley	1 tablespoon chopped parsley
2 hard-boiled eggs, coarsely chopped	2 hard-cooked eggs, coarsely chopped
50 g/2 oz salami or cooked ham, coarsely chopped	¼ cup coarsely chopped salami or processed ham
50 g/2 oz Gruyère cheese, coarsely chopped	¼ cup coarsely chopped Gruyère cheese
2 × 15 ml spoons/2 tablespoons olive oil	2 tablespoons olive oil
1 small onion, sliced	1 small onion, sliced
150 ml/¼ pint red wine	⅔ cup red wine
1 × 15 ml spoon/1 tablespoon tomato purée	1 tablespoon tomato paste
4 × 15 ml spoons/4 tablespoons hot water	¼ cup hot water

Beat the slice of beef with a rolling pin or mallet to flatten. Continue beating until the meat is about 5 mm/¼ inch thick and measures about 23 × 25 cm/9 × 10 inches. Season with salt and pepper.

Soak the bread in a little milk, and, when softened, squeeze it dry and beat it with a fork. Add the pork, beef, beaten eggs, Parmesan or Peconino cheese, parsley and salt and pepper to taste. Mix until thoroughly blended. Spread this mixture over the flattened beef to within 2.5 cm/1 inch of the edges.

Mix together the chopped eggs, salami or ham and the Gruyère cheese and arrange down the centre of the meat. Starting from the shorter edge, roll up neatly to form a thick sausage shape and tie securely with string.

Heat the oil in a large saucepan and sauté the onion for 5 minutes until soft. Put in the meat roll and sauté, turning occasionally, until lightly browned all over. Add the wine, tomato purée (paste) blended with the hot water, and salt and pepper. Cover tightly and simmer very gently for 1½ to 2 hours until tender, turning once and adding a little more hot water if too much of the liquid evaporates.

Transfer the meat roll to a carving board and remove the strings. Skim the fat off the pan juices then boil the juices rapidly until reduced and thickened. Carve the meat into thick slices, arrange on a warm serving plate and spoon over the sauce. Serve immediately.
SERVES 8

ESCALOPE MILANESE

METRIC/IMPERIAL	AMERICAN
6 × 100 g/4 oz veal escalopes	6 × 4 oz veal cutlets
50 g/2 oz plain flour	½ cup all-purpose flour
2 eggs, beaten	2 eggs, beaten
salt	salt
75 g/3 oz fresh breadcrumbs	1½ cups soft bread crumbs
300 ml/½ pint olive oil	1½ cups olive oil
2 lemons, cut into wedges to garnish	2 lemons, cut into wedges to garnish

Trim the veal and make a few cuts around the edges. Beat the veal with a rolling pin or mallet to flatten. Sieve the flour onto a plate. Mix the beaten egg with some salt on a second plate, and put the breadcrumbs on a third. Dip the veal first into the flour and shake off the excess. Dip the veal into the beaten eggs and finally into the breadcrumbs. Do not press the crumbs in, just shake off the excess.
Heat the oil in a frying pan (skillet) and sauté the veal escalopes, 2 at a time, for 2 minutes on each side, until golden brown. Drain on kitchen paper towels and keep hot until all escalopes have been cooked. Transfer to a warm serving plate, garnish with the lemon wedges and serve immediately.
SERVES 6

MEATBALLS CASALINGA

METRIC/IMPERIAL
300 ml/½ pint Tomato Sauce
   (see page 75)
50 g/2 oz crustless white bread
milk for soaking
450 g/1 lb pie veal or boneless
   leg of beef, trimmed and
   chopped
2 cloves garlic
small bunch of parsley
2 thin strips of lemon rind
2 eggs
25 g/1 oz grated Parmesan
   cheese
large pinch of grated nutmeg
salt
freshly ground black pepper
flour
olive oil

AMERICAN
1¼ cups Tomato Sauce (see
   page 75)
2 oz crustless white bread
milk for soaking
1 lb pie veal or boneless leg of
   beef, trimmed and chopped
2 cloves garlic
small bunch of parsley
2 thin strips of lemon rind
2 eggs
¼ cup grated Parmesan
   cheese
large pinch of grated nutmeg
salt
freshly ground black pepper
flour
olive oil

Prepare the tomato sauce. Soak the bread in a little milk and when softened squeeze to remove liquid. Pass the meat, bread, garlic, parsley and lemon rind through a fine mincer (grinder) twice. Beat in the eggs, cheese, nutmeg and salt and pepper to taste and mix thoroughly.

With well-floured hands, shape the mixture into small balls about 2.5 cm/1 inch in diameter then roll on a floured surface and flatten slightly with a knife. Handle as little as possible so that the meatballs remain light.

Heat olive oil in a large frying pan (skillet) to a depth of 5 mm/¼ inch. Sauté the meatballs in batches, for about 3 minutes on each side until crisp outside and cooked. Lift out and drain on crumpled kitchen paper towels.

While the meatballs are cooking, reheat the tomato sauce, diluting it with water to give a fairly thin consistency. Put in the meatballs, stirring gently and simmer for 20 minutes. Transfer to a warm serving dish and serve immediately.

SERVES 4

STUFFED VEAL ROLLS

METRIC/IMPERIAL	AMERICAN
8 veal escalopes, each weighing 50 g/2 oz	8 veal scaloppini, each weighing 2 oz
8 thin slices ham	8 thin slices processed ham
25 g/1 oz crustless bread	1 oz crustless bread
3 × 15 ml spoons/3 tablespoons sultanas	3 tablespoons raisins
25 g/1 oz pine nuts or blanched slivered almonds	¼ cup pine nuts or blanched slivered almonds
4 × 15 ml spoons/4 tablespoons grated Parmesan cheese	¼ cup grated Parmesan cheese
2 × 15 ml spoons/2 tablespoons chopped parsley	2 tablespoons chopped parsley
salt	salt
freshly ground black pepper	freshly ground black pepper
1 × 15 ml spoon/1 tablespoon olive oil	1 tablespoon olive oil
150 ml/¼ pint white wine	⅔ cup white wine

Lay the veal flat between greaseproof (waxed) paper and beat with a rolling pin or mallet until thin. Remove the paper and lay a slice of ham on each.

Soak the bread in water and then squeeze dry. Put into a bowl and add the sultanas (raisins), nuts, cheese, parsley and salt and pepper to taste. Mix well. Divide the stuffing between the slices of veal, roll up and secure with wooden cocktail sticks (toothpicks).

Heat the oil in a frying pan (skillet) and sauté the rolls over moderate heat turning until lightly browned all over. Pour in the wine, cover tightly and simmer very gently for 20 to 25 minutes until tender, turning once.

Transfer the rolls to a warm serving dish, and remove the sticks. Boil the pan juices until reduced by about half and thickened. Pour over the veal and serve immediately.

SERVES 4

OSSO BUCO

METRIC/IMPERIAL	AMERICAN
1 kg/2 lb shin of veal, cut into 4 pieces	2 lb shin of veal, cut into 4 pieces
salt	salt
freshly ground black pepper	freshly ground black pepper
25 g/1 oz butter	2 tablespoons butter
1 × 15 ml spoon/1 tablespoon oil	1 tablespoon oil
1 large onion, chopped	1 large onion, chopped
4 celery sticks, sliced	4 celery stalks, sliced
2 large carrots, sliced	2 large carrots, sliced
150 ml/¼ pint dry white wine	⅔ cup dry white wine
1 × 5 ml spoon/1 teaspoon lemon juice	1 teaspoon lemon juice
300 ml/½ pint stock	1¼ cups bouillon
1 × 2.5 ml spoon/½ teaspoon dried rosemary	½ teaspoon dried rosemary
1 × 400 g/14 oz can tomatoes	1 × 16 oz can tomatoes
2 × 5 ml spoons/2 teaspoons cornflour (optional)	2 teaspoons cornstarch (optional)
To garnish:	To garnish:
lemon rind	lemon zest
chopped parsley	chopped parsley

Season the veal with salt and pepper. Heat the butter and oil in a frying pan (skillet) and sauté the veal until browned all over. Remove from the pan.

Sauté the onion, celery and carrots for 5 minutes, then pour off the excess fat from the pan. Add the wine and lemon juice and return the veal to the pan. Bring to the boil, cover and simmer very gently for 45 minutes.

Add the stock (bouillon) rosemary and tomatoes and their juice. Bring to the boil, cover and simmer for a further 1 hour or until the meat is tender. Transfer the veal with a slotted spoon to a warm serving dish. If liked, thicken the sauce with the cornflour (cornstarch) blended with a little cold water and boil for 2 minutes.

Taste and adjust seasonings. Pour sauce over veal and sprinkle with a mixture of lemon rind (zest) and chopped parsley. Serve immediately.

SERVES 4

SAUTÉED VEAL

METRIC/IMPERIAL	AMERICAN
450 g/1 lb veal fillet	1 lb veal fillet
3 × 15 ml spoons/3 tablespoons olive oil	3 tablespoons olive oil
2 cloves garlic, crushed	2 cloves garlic, crushed
1 bay leaf	1 bay leaf
6 fresh sage leaves, chopped	6 fresh sage leaves, chopped
salt	salt
freshly ground black pepper	freshly ground black pepper
5 × 15 ml spoons/5 tablespoons dry white wine	1/3 cup dry white wine

Sautéed Veal; Stuffed Breast of Veal Genovese

Slice the veal thinly, then beat it out with a rolling pin or mallet as thinly as possible. Cut into 2.5 cm/1 inch square pieces.

Heat the oil in a large heavy frying pan (skillet) and sauté the garlic and sage leaves over low heat for 1 minute. Remove from the heat, add the meat and stir until all the pieces are well coated with oil. Return to a moderately high heat and cook for 3 to 4 minutes, stirring constantly, until the veal is just cooked. Season with salt and pepper, lift out the meat with a slotted spoon and discard the bay leaf. Transfer the meat to a serving dish and keep warm whilst preparing the sauce.

Add the wine to the frying pan (skillet) and boil briskly, scraping up the juices from the base of the pan, until reduced to a small quantity of syrupy sauce. Spoon over the meat and serve immediately.

SERVES 4

STUFFED BREAST OF VEAL GENOVESE

METRIC/IMPERIAL	AMERICAN
1 kg/2 lb piece of boned breast of veal, beaten 5 mm/1/4 inch thick, plus bones	2 lb piece of boned breast of veal, beaten 1/4 inch thick, plus bones
salt	salt
freshly ground black pepper	freshly ground black pepper
50 g/2 oz crustless bread	2 oz crustless bread
milk for soaking	milk for soaking
100 g/4 oz veal sweetbreads	1/4 lb veal sweetbreads
25 g/1 oz butter	2 tablespoons butter
1 small onion, finely chopped	1 small onion, finely chopped
350 g/12 oz finely minced pork	1 1/2 cups finely ground pork
40 g/1 1/2 oz grated Parmesan cheese	1/3 cup grated Parmesan cheese
1/2 × 2.5 ml spoon/1/4 teaspoon dried marjoram	1/4 teaspoon dried marjoram
75 g/3 oz peas	1/2 cup peas
1 artichoke heart, chopped	1 artichoke heart, chopped
25 g/1 oz shelled pistachio nuts	1/4 cup shelled pistachio nuts
2 eggs, lightly beaten	2 eggs, lightly beaten
2 hard-boiled eggs	2 hard-cooked eggs

Lay the veal flat, season with salt and pepper, fold in half and sew the two longer sides together with thread to form a pocket. Soak the bread in the milk until softened, then squeeze dry. Cover the sweetbreads with cold water, bring to the boil and simmer for 10 minutes. Drain and chop.

Melt the butter in a saucepan and sauté the onion for 5 minutes until soft. Remove from the heat and add the sweetbreads, bread, pork, cheese, marjoram, peas, artichoke heart, pistachio nuts, beaten eggs and salt and pepper. Mix together lightly but thoroughly.

Spread half of the stuffing in the veal pocket, arrange the hard-boiled (hard-cooked) eggs on top, and cover with the remaining stuffing. Carefully sew up the opening to enclose the stuffing.

Put the veal bones in a deep saucepan, lay the meat roll on top and cover with cold salted water. Bring to the boil, cover and simmer gently for 1 1/2 to 2 hours. Leave to cool in the water, then drain. Place in the refrigerator. When cold, transfer to a serving plate and cut into fairly thick slices. Serve immediately.

SERVES 10 TO 12

VEAL CROQUETTES WITH MUSHROOM SAUCE

METRIC/IMPERIAL	AMERICAN
350 g/12 oz lean pie veal	¾ lb boneless veal for stew
1 onion, chopped	1 onion, chopped
225 g/8 oz sausagemeat	1 cup sausagemeat
salt	salt
freshly ground black pepper	freshly ground black pepper
Tabasco sauce	Tabasco sauce
½ × 2.5 ml spoon/¼ teaspoon ground mace	¼ teaspoon ground mace
1 egg, beaten	1 egg, beaten
50 g/2 oz fresh breadcrumbs	1 cup fresh bread crumbs
2 × 15 ml spoons/2 tablespoons oil	2 tablespoons oil
50 g/2 oz butter	¼ cup butter
1 onion, finely sliced	1 onion, finely sliced
100 g/4 oz mushrooms, sliced	1 cup sliced mushrooms
300 ml/½ pint stock	1¼ cups bouillon
salt	salt
freshly ground black pepper	freshly ground black pepper
Tabasco sauce	Tabasco sauce
2 × 5 ml spoons/2 teaspoons cornflour	2 teaspoons cornstarch
3 × 15 ml spoons/3 tablespoons soured cream (optional)	3 tablespoons sour cream

Finely mince (grind) the veal and onion in a mincer (grinder). Mix in the sausagemeat with salt, pepper, Tabasco, mace and half the beaten egg. Divide into four and form into flat triangle shapes. Place the remaining beaten egg on one plate and the breadcrumbs on another. Dip the croquettes first in egg, then in breadcrumbs, shaking off any excess.

Melt the oil and half the butter in a frying pan (skillet) and sauté the croquettes for 10 to 12 minutes each side, until cooked and browned. Drain on kitchen paper towels and arrange on a warm serving dish. Keep warm.

Meanwhile, make the sauce: melt the remaining butter in a small saucepan and sauté the onion for 5 minutes until soft. Add the mushrooms and sauté for 3 minutes. Add the stock (bouillon), salt and pepper and Tabasco sauce and bring to the boil. Simmer the sauce for 10 minutes then thicken with the cornflour (cornstarch) blended with a little cold water, and return to the boil for 2 minutes.

Taste and adjust the seasoning. Stir in the cream, if using. Reheat gently and serve immediately with the croquettes.
SERVES 4

VITELLO TONNATO

METRIC/IMPERIAL	AMERICAN
750 g/1½ lb boned leg of veal, rolled	1½ lb boned leg of veal, rolled
1 bay leaf	1 bay leaf
6 peppercorns	6 peppercorns
1 carrot, sliced	1 carrot, sliced
1 onion, sliced	1 onion, sliced
2 celery sticks, chopped	2 celery stalks, chopped
stock or water	bouillon or water
½ × 198 g/7 oz can tuna	½ × 7 oz can tuna
1 × 50 g/1¾ oz can anchovy fillets, drained	1 × 2 oz can anchovy fillets, drained
150 ml/¼ pint olive oil	⅔ cup olive oil
2 egg yolks	2 egg yolks
1 × 15 ml spoon/1 tablespoon lemon juice	1 tablespoon lemon juice
salt	salt
freshly ground black pepper	freshly ground black pepper
To garnish:	To garnish:
capers	capers
lemon slices	lemon slices
parsley sprigs	parsley sprigs

Place the veal in a saucepan with the bay leaf, peppercorns, carrot, onion, celery and stock (bouillon) or water to cover. Bring to the boil, skim off the scum, cover and simmer gently for 1 hour or until tender. Drain and cool.

Meanwhile, mash the tuna fish with 4 anchovy fillets and 1 × 15 ml spoon/1 tablespoon oil. Add the egg yolks and either press through a sieve or blend in an electric blender until smooth. Stir in the lemon juice and gradually beat in the remaining oil, a little at a time, until the sauce is smooth and has the consistency of thin cream. Season.

Slice the veal thinly and arrange in a shallow dish. Coat with the sauce, cover the dish and chill overnight in the refrigerator. To serve, garnish with the remaining anchovies, capers, lemon slices, and parsley.
SERVES 6

VEAL AND APPLE RISSOLES

METRIC/IMPERIAL	AMERICAN
2 apples, peeled, cored and finely chopped	2 apples, peeled, cored and finely chopped
450 g/1 lb minced veal	2 cups ground veal
1 egg, beaten	1 egg, beaten
salt	salt
freshly ground black pepper	freshly ground black pepper
50 g/2 oz plain flour	½ cup all-purpose flour
65 g/2½ oz butter	5 tablespoons butter
4 × 15 ml spoons/4 tablespoons red wine	¼ cup red wine

Put apples, veal and egg in a bowl with salt and pepper to taste. Mix well, adding a little flour to bind. Shape the mixture into rissoles and coat with flour.

Melt the butter in a large frying pan (skillet), add the rissoles and fry over moderate heat until browned on all sides. Add the wine, cover and cook gently for a further 15 minutes. Serve immediately.
SERVES 4

CREAMY VEAL OLIVES

METRIC/IMPERIAL
4 small veal escalopes
salt
freshly ground black pepper
2 slices cooked ham, halved
2 hard-boiled eggs, halved
50 g/2 oz butter
300 ml/½ pint stock
2 × 15 ml spoons/2
    tablespoons dry white wine
    (optional)
100 g/4 oz mushrooms,
    quartered
1 × 15 ml spoon/1 tablespoon
    plain flour
4 × 15 ml spoons/4
    tablespoons double cream
chopped parsley to garnish

AMERICAN
4 small veal cutlets
salt
freshly ground black pepper
2 slices processed ham, halved
2 hard-cooked eggs, halved
¼ cup butter
1¼ cups bouillon
2 tablespoons dry white wine
    (optional)
1 cup mushrooms, quartered
1 tablespoon all-purpose flour
4 tablespoons heavy cream
chopped parsley to garnish

Beat the veal with a rolling pin or mallet to flatten. Season with salt and pepper. Place half a slice of ham and half an egg on each one; roll up and secure with wooden cocktail sticks (toothpicks). Heat 25 g/1 oz (2 tablespoons) butter in a frying pan (skillet) and sauté the veal olives until browned all over. Transfer to a shallow casserole. Pour on the stock (bouillon) and wine, if using, cover and place in a preheated moderate oven (180°C/350°F, Gas Mark 4) and cook for 1 hour. Drain off the liquid and reserve. Transfer the veal olives to a warm serving dish, remove cocktail sticks (toothpicks) and keep hot.

Melt the remaining butter in a saucepan and sauté the mushrooms for 2 minutes. Stir in the flour and cook for 1 minute. Gradually add the cooking liquid and bring to the boil. Season to taste and simmer for 2 minutes. Stir in the cream and reheat gently without boiling. Pour over the olives, garnish with parsley and serve immediately.
SERVES 4

Vitello Tonnato; Creamy Veal Olives; Veal Croquettes with Mushroom Sauce

SAUTÉED VEAL KIDNEYS

METRIC/IMPERIAL	AMERICAN
1 × 15 ml spoon/1 tablespoon oil	1 tablespoon oil
25 g/1 oz butter	2 tablespoons butter
1 large clove garlic, halved	1 large clove garlic, halved
450 g/1 lb veal kidneys, cleaned and thinly sliced	1 lb veal kidneys, cleaned and thinly sliced
2 × 15 ml spoons/2 tablespoons chopped parsley	2 tablespoons chopped parsley
juice of ½ large lemon	juice of ½ large lemon
salt	salt
freshly ground black pepper	freshly ground black pepper
small triangles crisp fried bread to garnish	small triangles crisp fried bread to garnish

Heat the oil and butter in a frying pan (skillet) and sauté the garlic for 2 minutes. Discard the garlic.

Increase the heat, and when the fat is hot add the kidney slices and sauté over moderate heat, stirring constantly for 2 minutes. Stir in the parsley and continue cooking and stirring for 2 minutes. Add the lemon juice and cook for 2 minutes, until the kidney slices are tender but still juicy and slightly pink in the centre, and the liquid is syrupy.

Season with salt and pepper. Transfer to a warm serving plate. Garnish with bread and serve immediately.
SERVES 4

TRIPE GENOVESE

METRIC/IMPERIAL	AMERICAN
1 kg/2 lb dressed tripe, cut into strips	2 lb dressed tripe, cut into strips
4 × 15 ml spoons/4 tablespoons olive oil	¼ cup olive oil
25 g/1 oz butter	2 tablespoons butter
1 onion, peeled and chopped	1 onion, peeled and chopped
1 celery stalk, chopped	1 celery stalk, chopped
1 carrot, peeled and chopped	1 carrot, peeled and chopped
75 g/3 oz mushrooms, chopped	1 cup chopped mushrooms
salt	salt
freshly ground black pepper	freshly ground black pepper
450 g/1 lb tomatoes, skinned finely chopped	2 cups tomatoes, skinned and finely chopped
450 g/1 lb potatoes, peeled and cut into pieces	1 lb potatoes, peeled and cut into pieces

Blanch the tripe in boiling water for 5 minutes, drain, then plunge into cold water.

Heat the oil and butter in a flameproof casserole, add the chopped vegetables and fry gently for 5 minutes. Drain the tripe and add to the casserole with salt and pepper to taste. Cook for 15 minutes, stirring frequently.

Add the tomatoes and 7 tablespoons warm water. Cover and simmer for 30 minutes. Add the potatoes and cook for a further 30 minutes, stirring once or twice. Serve immediately.
SERVES 6

SWEETBREADS NAPOLETANA

METRIC/IMPERIAL	AMERICAN
2 × 15 ml spoons/2 tablespoons olive oil	2 tablespoons olive oil
750 g/1½ lb veal sweetbreads, cleaned and sliced	1½ lb veal sweetbreads, cleaned and sliced
300 ml/½ pint milk	1¼ cups milk
4 slices of toast	4 slices of toast
75 g/3 oz mixed grated Parmesan and Cheddar cheese	¾ cup grated Parmesan and Cheddar cheese, mixed
salt	salt
paprika pepper	paprika pepper
50 g/2 oz mushrooms, sliced	½ cup sliced mushrooms
25 g/1 oz butter	2 tablespoons butter

Heat the oil in a frying pan (skillet) and sauté the sweetbreads for 2 minutes, stirring. Remove from the heat. Put 1 × 15 ml spoon/1 tablespoon milk into an ovenproof dish and lay in the slices of toast.

Mix the remaining milk with the cheese, salt and paprika and spread over the toast. Lay the sweetbreads on top and add the sliced mushrooms. Dot with butter. Cover and place in a preheated moderate oven (180°C/350°F, Gas Mark 4) and cook for 20 minutes. Serve immediately, from the dish.
SERVES 4

LIVER POMODORO

METRIC/IMPERIAL	AMERICAN
25 g/1 oz butter	2 tablespoons butter
350 g/12 oz lambs' liver, cut into 1 cm/½ inch strips	¾ lb lamb liver, cut into ½ inch strips
4 bacon rashers, chopped	4 bacon slices, chopped
25 g/1 oz plain flour	¼ cup all-purpose flour
300 ml/½ pint stock	1¼ cups bouillon
8–12 spring onions, trimmed	8–12 scallions, trimmed
1 × 200 g/7 oz can tomatoes	1 × 7 oz can tomatoes
salt	salt
freshly ground black pepper	freshly ground black pepper

Melt the butter in a frying pan (skillet) and sauté the liver and bacon for 2 minutes. Remove from the pan and drain on kitchen paper towels. Add the flour to remaining fat in the pan and cook for 1 minute, stirring.

Remove the pan from the heat and gradually stir in the stock (bouillon). Return to the heat and bring to the boil, stirring. Return liver and bacon to the pan, add spring onions (scallions), tomatoes with their juice and salt and pepper to taste. Simmer gently for 15 minutes, stirring occasionally. Transfer to a warm serving dish and serve immediately.
SERVES 4

Roman Liver

ROMAN LIVER

METRIC/IMPERIAL
750 g/1½ lb pig's liver, sliced
25 g/1 oz seasoned plain flour
25 g/1 oz butter
1 × 15 ml spoon/1 tablespoon
   oil
1 medium onion, chopped
1 × 2.5 ml spoon/½ teaspoon
   dried oregano
1 × 400 g/14 oz can tomatoes
salt
freshly ground black pepper

AMERICAN
1½ lb pork liver, sliced
4 tablespoons seasoned all-
   purpose flour
2 tablespoons butter
1 tablespoon oil
1 medium onion, chopped
1 teaspoon dried oregano
1 × 16 oz can tomatoes
salt
freshly ground black pepper

Coat the liver in seasoned flour, shaking off any excess. Heat the butter and oil in a frying pan (skillet) and sauté the onion for 5 minutes until soft. Add the liver and sauté until browned. Sprinkle over the oregano and stir in the tomatoes and their juice. Season with salt and pepper. Cover and simmer for 20 to 25 minutes until cooked.

Transfer to a warm serving dish and serve immediately.
SERVES 4

SALADS AND VEGETABLES

SWEET PEPPERS WITH TUNA AND CAPERS

METRIC/IMPERIAL	AMERICAN
6 large red, yellow and/or green peppers	6 large red, yellow and/or green peppers
4 × 15 ml spoons/4 tablespoons olive oil	¼ cup olive oil
1 × 5 ml spoon/1 teaspoon lemon juice	1 teaspoon lemon juice
1 clove garlic, crushed	1 clove garlic, crushed
salt	salt
freshly ground black pepper	freshly ground black pepper
1 × 200 g/7 oz can tuna, drained and flaked	1 × 7 oz can tuna, drained and flaked
1 × 15 ml spoon/1 tablespoon capers	1 tablespoon capers
parsley sprigs to garnish	parsley sprigs to garnish

Place the peppers under a preheated moderate grill (broiler) and heat for 10 minutes, turning from time to time, until the skins are charred and blistered all over. When cool enough to handle, peel off the skins, then cut each pepper lengthwise into three strips and discard the seeds. Rinse under cold water to remove all traces of skin and seeds.

Put the strips in a bowl with the oil, lemon juice, garlic and a little salt and pepper. Leave to marinate for 30 minutes, stirring occasionally. Drain, reserving the marinade. Lay the pepper strips flat.

Mix the tuna and capers together. Place a generous spoonful on each pepper strip and roll up. Arrange the rolls in a shallow serving dish with the colours alternating. Pour the marinade over, garnish with parsley and serve immediately.

SERVES 6

CAULIFLOWER SALAD

METRIC/IMPERIAL	AMERICAN
1 large cauliflower, broken into florets	1 large cauliflower, broken into florets
salt	salt
juice of ½ lemon	juice of ½ lemon
freshly ground black pepper	freshly ground black pepper
4–5 × 15 ml spoons/4–5 tablespoons olive oil	¼–⅓ cup olive oil
6 anchovy fillets, finely chopped	6 anchovy fillets, finely chopped
1 × 15 ml spoon/1 tablespoon drained capers	1 tablespoon drained capers
1 × 15 ml spoon/1 tablespoon chopped parsley	1 tablespoon chopped parsley
50 g/2 oz black olives	⅓ cup ripe olives

Cook the cauliflower florets in a large pan of boiling salted water for 5 minutes until just tender but still quite firm. Drain, rinse under cold water and drain again.

Mix the lemon juice, salt and pepper and the oil together in a salad bowl. Add the cauliflower and toss gently to coat with the dressing. Sprinkle with the anchovies, capers and parsley and surround with the olives. Serve immediately.

SERVES 4

Sweet Peppers with Tuna and Capers; Cauliflower Salad

STUFFED COURGETTES (ZUCCHINI)

METRIC/IMPERIAL	AMERICAN
6 courgettes, trimmed	6 zucchini, trimmed
salt	salt
25 g/1 oz crustless white bread	1 oz crustless white bread
milk for soaking	milk for soaking
100 g/4 oz Ricotta or soft curd cheese	½ cup Ricotta or soft curd cheese
½ × 2.5 ml spoon/¼ teaspoon dried oregano	¼ teaspoon dried oregano
1 clove garlic, crushed	1 clove garlic, crushed
40 g/1½ oz grated Parmesan cheese	⅓ cup grated Parmesan cheese
1 egg yolk	1 egg yolk
freshly ground black pepper	freshly ground black pepper

Cook the courgettes (zucchini) in a large pan of boiling salted water for 5 minutes, then drain. Meanwhile, soak the bread in milk until softened. Squeeze dry. Cut the courgettes (zucchini) in half lengthwise and scoop out the centres, using a teaspoon, leaving long boat-shaped cases for filling.

Chop the courgette (zucchini) centres finely, put into a bowl and add the bread, Ricotta, oregano, garlic, Parmesan, egg yolk, pepper and salt. Mix thoroughly. The consistency should be fairly soft; if too stiff, add a little milk.

Fill the courgette (zucchini) cases and spread the stuffing flat. Arrange close together in a single layer in a well oiled shallow baking tray or dish.

Place in a preheated moderately hot oven (190°C/375°F, Gas Mark 5) and cook for 35 to 40 minutes until the courgettes (zucchini) are tender and the filling is golden brown. Serve immediately.

SERVES 3 TO 4

SPINACH OMELETTE

METRIC/IMPERIAL	AMERICAN
225 g/8 oz fresh spinach	½ lb fresh spinach
salt	salt
freshly ground black pepper	freshly ground black pepper
pinch of ground nutmeg	pinch of ground nutmeg
25 g/1 oz butter	2 tablespoons butter
3 eggs	3 eggs

Wash the spinach and cook with the water that clings to the leaves in a covered pan for 3 minutes. Drain, squeeze and coarsely chop the spinach. Season with salt, pepper and nutmeg. Melt half the butter in a saucepan and sauté spinach very gently, stirring frequently, for 5 minutes.

Break the eggs into a basin, season lightly and beat with a fork. Stir in the spinach, mixing well.

Melt the remaining butter in a heavy 18 cm/7 inch frying pan (skillet) and pour in the egg mixture. Cook over high heat for 2 minutes or until lightly set, then toss or turn with a fish slice and cook the underside for a few seconds. Invert onto a warm plate and serve immediately.

SERVES 1

GENOESE SALAD

METRIC/IMPERIAL	AMERICAN
1 × 425 g/15 oz can cannellini beans	1 × 16 oz can cannellini beans
100 g/4 oz thinly sliced salami	¼ lb thinly sliced salami
225 g/8 oz Lancashire cheese, crumbled	1½ cups crumbled Lancashire cheese
olive oil	olive oil
salt	salt
freshly ground black pepper	freshly ground black pepper

Drain the beans well and place them in a salad bowl. Add the salami and sprinkle the cheese over the top. Pour a little oil over and season with salt and pepper. Serve immediately.

SERVES 4

RAW MUSHROOM SALAD

METRIC/IMPERIAL
225 g/8 oz mushrooms
1 clove garlic, halved
5 × 15 ml spoons/5
    tablespoons olive oil
2 × 15 ml spoons/2
    tablespoons lemon juice
freshly ground black pepper
salt
few sprigs of parsley, roughly
    chopped
175 g/6 oz peeled prawns or 8
    anchovy fillets, finely
    chopped (optional)

AMERICAN
2 cups mushrooms
1 clove garlic
⅓ cup olive oil
2 tablespoons lemon juice
freshly ground black pepper
salt
few sprigs of parsley, roughly
    chopped
1 cup shelled shrimp or 8
    anchovy fillets, finely
    chopped (optional)

Wipe but do not peel the mushrooms and slice thinly. Rub the cut surfaces of the garlic around a mixing bowl.

Beat the olive oil, lemon juice and pepper together in the bowl. Add the mushrooms and toss gently to mix thoroughly with the dressing. Cover with plastic wrap and refrigerate for 1 hour.

Add the salt and roughly chopped parsley and toss again. Divide between 4 individual dishes and, if using, scatter the prawns (shrimp) or anchovies over the top. Serve immediately.
SERVES 4

Spinach Omelette; Raw Mushroom Salad; Stuffed Courgettes

CORN AND PASTA SALAD

METRIC/IMPERIAL	AMERICAN
225 g/8 oz pasta shells	½ lb pasta shells
salt	salt
3 × 15 ml spoons/3 tablespoons olive oil	3 tablespoons olive oil
1 × 15 ml spoon/1 tablespoon wine vinegar	1 tablespoon wine vinegar
1 × 198 g/7 oz can tuna	1 × 7 oz can tuna
1 × 5 ml spoon/1 teaspoon grated lemon rind	1 teaspoon grated lemon rind
1 clove garlic, crushed	1 clove garlic, crushed
2 celery sticks, sliced	2 celery stalks, sliced
1 onion, thinly sliced	1 onion, thinly sliced
1 × 198 g/7 oz can sweetcorn, drained	1 × 7 oz can whole kernel corn, drained
freshly ground black pepper	freshly ground black pepper
25 g/1 oz butter	2 tablespoons butter
50 g/2 oz mushrooms, sliced	½ cup sliced mushrooms
50 g/2 oz French beans, cooked	50 g/2 oz green beans, cooked
chopped parsley to garnish	chopped parsley to garnish

Cook the pasta shells in a large saucepan of boiling salted water for 10 minutes until tender but *al dente*. Drain and cool. Put the oil and wine vinegar into a bowl. Add the oil from the tuna, lemon rind and garlic and stir well. Flake the tuna and add to the oil mixture with the celery, onion, corn and pasta shells and toss together, adding salt and pepper to taste. Chill in the refrigerator.

Melt the butter in a small saucepan and sauté the mushrooms for 3 minutes. Allow to cool. Transfer the salad to a serving dish. Arrange the sliced mushrooms and beans on top. Garnish with chopped parsley and serve immediately.

SERVES 4 TO 6

CABBAGE WITH BACON

METRIC/IMPERIAL	AMERICAN
4 streaky bacon rashers, diced	4 fatty bacon slices, diced
1 clove garlic, crushed	1 clove garlic, crushed
1 sprig of rosemary	1 sprig of rosemary
1 medium savoy cabbage, shredded	1 medium savoy cabbage, shredded
150 ml/¼ pint chicken stock	⅔ cup chicken bouillon
salt	salt
freshly ground black pepper	freshly ground black pepper

Put the bacon, garlic and rosemary in a heavy based frying pan (skillet) and sauté over moderate heat for 5 minutes until browned.

Lower the heat and add the shredded cabbage, stock (bouillon) and salt and pepper to taste. Cover and cook gently for 40 minutes, stirring frequently. Transfer to a warmed serving dish and serve immediately.

SERVES 4 TO 6

Courgettes and Tomato; Cabbage with Bacon

COURGETTES (ZUCCHINI) AND TOMATO

METRIC/IMPERIAL	AMERICAN
750 g/1½ lb courgettes, sliced	1½ lb zucchini, sliced
salt	salt
2 × 15 ml spoons/2 tablespoons olive oil	2 tablespoons olive oil
1 small onion, chopped	1 small onion, chopped
1 clove garlic, crushed	1 clove garlic, crushed
450 g/1 lb tomatoes, peeled and sliced	2 cups skinned, sliced tomatoes
2 × 15 ml spoons/2 tablespoons wine vinegar	2 tablespoons wine vinegar
1 × 15 ml spoon/1 tablespoon lemon juice	1 tablespoon lemon juice
1 × 15 ml spoon/1 tablespoon caster sugar	1 tablespoon superfine sugar
freshly ground black pepper	freshly ground black pepper

Sprinkle the courgettes (zucchini) with salt and toss lightly. Leave to drain for 1 hour. Shake the courgettes (zucchini) in a cloth to dry. Heat the oil in a large frying pan (skillet) and sauté the onion and garlic for 5 minutes until soft. Add the courgettes (zucchini) and cook gently, stirring occasionally, for about 10 to 15 minutes. When they are soft, add the tomatoes. Stir in the vinegar, lemon juice and sugar. Add salt and pepper to taste and cook for a further 5 minutes. Transfer to a warm serving dish and serve immediately.

SERVES 4

COURGETTE (ZUCCHINI) NEAPOLITAN

METRIC/IMPERIAL	AMERICAN
450 g/1 lb tomatoes, peeled and chopped	2 cups skinned, chopped tomatoes
1 small onion, chopped	1 small onion, chopped
salt	salt
freshly ground black pepper	freshly ground black pepper
750 g/1½ lb courgettes, chopped	1½ lb zucchini, chopped
2 × 15 ml spoons/2 tablespoons plain flour	2 tablespoons all-purpose flour
25 g/1 oz butter	2 tablespoons butter
225 g/8 oz Edam cheese, thinly sliced	½ lb Edam cheese, thinly sliced

Put the tomatoes and onion in a saucepan, season with salt and pepper and cook for 10 minutes, stirring, until thick.

Coat the courgettes (zucchini) in flour, shaking off any excess. Melt the butter in a large frying pan (skillet) and sauté the courgettes (zucchini) until brown. Make alternate layers of courgette (zucchini), the tomato mixture and the cheese in a shallow casserole, finishing with a layer of cheese. Place in a preheated moderately hot oven (190°C/375°F, Gas Mark 5) and bake for 30 minutes. Serve immediately.

SERVES 4

STUFFED AUBERGINES (EGGPLANT)

METRIC/IMPERIAL	AMERICAN
2 medium-sized aubergines, trimmed	2 medium-sized eggplant, trimmed
salt	salt
olive oil	olive oil
1 × 50 g/1¾ oz can anchovies, drained and chopped	1 × 2 oz can anchovies, drained and chopped
1 × 15 ml spoon/1 tablespoon chopped parsley	1 tablespoon chopped parsley
1 × 15 ml spoon/1 tablespoon grated onion	1 tablespoon minced onion
1 tomato, peeled and chopped	1 tomato, skinned and chopped
50 g/2 oz fresh breadcrumbs	1 cup fresh bread crumbs
freshly ground black pepper	freshly ground black pepper

Cut the aubergines (eggplant) in half lengthwise. Cut around each half, 5 mm/¼ inch from the skin, and then criss-cross cut the surface lightly to ensure even cooking. Sprinkle with salt and olive oil and place in a greased ovenproof dish. Place in a preheated moderately hot oven (190°C/375°F, Gas Mark 5) and cook for 15 to 20 minutes, until the centre is almost cooked.

Meanwhile, mix together the anchovies, parsley, onion, tomato, breadcrumbs and pepper to taste for the stuffing. Scoop out the flesh from the centre of the cooked aubergines (eggplant), chop and add to the stuffing. Fill the cases, mounding up the stuffing. Brush with oil and return to the oven for a further 15 minutes. Transfer to a warm serving dish and serve immediately.

SERVES 4

AUBERGINE (EGGPLANT) PIE

METRIC/IMPERIAL	AMERICAN
600 ml/1 pint Tomato Sauce (see page 75)	2½ cups Tomato Sauce (see page 75)
1 kg/2 lb aubergines, peeled	2 lb eggplant, peeled
salt	salt
flour	flour
5–8 × 15 ml spoons/5–8 tablespoons olive oil	⅓–½ cup olive oil
175 g/6 oz Mozzarella or Bel Paese cheese, thinly sliced	6 oz Mozzarella or Bel Paese cheese, thinly sliced
50 g/2 oz grated Parmesan cheese	½ cup grated Parmesan cheese

Prepare the tomato sauce. Cut the aubergines (eggplants) lengthwise into 5 mm/¼ inch slices. Place in a colander with a generous sprinkling of salt between each layer, cover and leave to drain for 1 hour. Press each slice between kitchen paper towels to dry thoroughly. Dust lightly with flour.

Heat about 3 × 15 ml spoons/3 tablespoons oil in a large frying pan (skillet). Sauté a single layer of aubergine (eggplant) slices over a moderately high heat until lightly browned on both sides. Drain on kitchen paper towels. Sauté the remaining aubergine (eggplant) slices, a few at a time, adding more oil as necessary.

Oil a shallow casserole. Cover the bottom with a thin layer of tomato sauce and add a layer of fried aubergine (eggplant) slices. Spoon over more tomato sauce, top with cheese slices and sprinkle with Parmesan. Repeat the layers until all the aubergine (eggplant) is used, ending with a layer of cheese and a good sprinkling of Parmesan.

Place in the centre of a preheated moderately hot oven (200°C/400°F, Gas Mark 6) and bake for 25 to 30 minutes, until bubbling hot and golden. Serve immediately.

SERVES 6

ITALIAN RATATOUILLE FLAN

METRIC/IMPERIAL	AMERICAN
Pastry:	Dough:
100 g/4 oz plain flour	1 cup all-purpose flour
salt	salt
50 g/2 oz margarine	¼ cup margarine
2 × 15 ml spoons/2 tablespoons water	2 tablespoons water
Filling:	Filling:
50 g/2 oz butter	¼ cup butter
100 g/4 oz aubergine, sliced	1 cup sliced eggplant
100 g/4 oz courgettes, sliced	1 cup sliced zucchini
100 g/4 oz tomatoes, peeled and chopped	½ cup skinned, chopped tomatoes
1 onion, chopped	1 onion, chopped
1 small green pepper, seeded and sliced	1 small green pepper, seeded and sliced
4 bacon rashers, chopped	4 bacon slices, chopped
freshly ground black pepper	freshly ground black pepper
100 g/4 oz Cheddar cheese, grated	1 cup grated Cheddar cheese

Sieve the flour and salt into a bowl and rub (cut) in the margarine until the mixture resembles fine breadcrumbs. Add enough water to make a stiff dough. Roll out the dough on a lightly floured surface and use to line a 19 cm/7½ inch flan dish.

Meanwhile, sprinkle salt on the aubergine (eggplant) slices and leave to drain in a colander for 1 hour. Pat dry with kitchen towels.

Melt the butter in a pan and sauté the aubergine (eggplant), courgettes (zucchini), tomatoes, onion, pepper and bacon until just tender. Add salt and pepper to taste and leave until cold. Spoon the vegetables into the flan and cover the top with foil. Place in a preheated moderately hot oven (200°C/400°F, Gas Mark 6) and cook for 15 minutes. Remove foil, pile cheese on top of the vegetables and cook for a further 15 minutes or until cheese is golden brown. Serve immediately.

SERVES 4

TOMATO SAUCE

METRIC/IMPERIAL
2 × 15 ml spoons/2
    tablespoons oil
1 clove garlic, halved
1 × 400 g/14 oz can tomatoes
1 × 15 ml spoon/ tablespoon
    tomato purée
2 × 5 ml spoons/2 teaspoons
    sugar
salt
freshly ground black pepper

AMERICAN
2 tablespoons oil
1 clove garlic, halved
1 × 14 oz can tomatoes
1 tablespoon tomato paste
2 teaspoons sugar
salt
freshly ground black pepper

Heat the oil in a saucepan over low heat, add the garlic and sauté for 5 minutes. Discard the garlic.

Add the tomatoes and their liquid, tomato purée (paste), sugar and salt and pepper to taste. Bring to the boil, cover and simmer very gently for 1 hour.

Beat the sauce if necessary to break up any large pieces of tomato, adjust the seasoning and use as required.
MAKES 300 ml/½ pint (1¼ cups)

Tomato Sauce

ARTICHOKE HEARTS WITH SPINACH

METRIC/IMPERIAL	AMERICAN
6 × 15 ml spoons/6 tablespoons olive oil	6 tablespoons olive oil
1 small onion, finely chopped	1 small onion, finely chopped
1 clove garlic, crushed	1 clove garlic, crushed
4 anchovies, drained and crushed	4 anchovies, drained and crushed
1 kg/2 lb spinach, finely chopped	2 lb spinach, finely chopped
25 g/1 oz plain flour	¼ cup all-purpose flour
salt	salt
freshly ground black pepper	freshly ground black pepper
8 globe artichokes	8 globe artichokes
50 g/2 oz dried breadcrumbs	½ cup dried bread crumbs
50 g/2 oz grated Parmesan cheese	½ cup grated Parmesan cheese

Heat half the oil in a large heavy based saucepan. Sauté the onion, garlic and anchovies for 5 minutes until the onion is soft. Add the spinach and cook for 2 minutes. Stir in the flour and salt and pepper to taste. Cover and cook gently for 5 minutes.

Clean the artichokes, discarding the hard outer leaves, spikes and chokes. Stand them close together in an oiled ovenproof dish, then cover with spinach. Sprinkle with the remaining oil, breadcrumbs, cheese and pepper to taste. Place in a preheated moderately hot oven (200°C/400°F, Gas Mark 6) and bake for 20 minutes. Serve immediately.
SERVES 4 OR 8

ITALIAN-STYLE CAULIFLOWER

METRIC/IMPERIAL	AMERICAN
1 large cauliflower	1 large cauliflower
salt	salt
25 g/1 oz butter	2 tablespoons, butter
1 medium onion, chopped	1 medium onion, chopped
1 clove garlic, crushed	1 clove garlic, crushed
350 g/12 oz tomatoes, peeled and chopped	1½ cups skinned, chopped tomatoes
1 × 15 ml spoon/1 tablespoon chopped parsley	1 tablespoon chopped parsley
25 g/1 oz grated Parmesan cheese	¼ cup grated Parmesan cheese
Cheese sauce:	Cheese sauce
50 g/2 oz butter	¼ cup butter
50 g/2 oz plain flour	½ cup all-purpose flour
600 ml/1 pint milk	2½ cups milk
salt	salt
cayenne pepper	cayenne pepper
175 g/6 oz Cheddar cheese, finely grated	1½ cups finely grated Cheddar cheese

Cook the cauliflower in a large pan of boiling salted water until tender. Meanwhile, melt the butter in a pan and sauté the onion and garlic for 5 minutes until soft. Add the tomatoes and parsley.

To make the cheese sauce: melt the butter in a pan, add the flour and cook for 1 minute. Remove from the heat and gradually stir in the milk. Return to the heat and bring to the boil, stirring. Cook for 1 minute and then remove from the heat. Add salt and pepper to taste and Cheddar cheese, and stir until the cheese has melted.

Drain the cauliflower and place in a flameproof dish. Spoon the tomato mixture over the cauliflower and coat with the cheese sauce. Sprinkle with Parmesan cheese and place under a preheated hot grill (broiler) until browned on top. Serve immediately.
SERVES 4 TO 6

PEAS WITH PROSCUITTO

METRIC/IMPERIAL
25 g/1 oz butter
1 small onion, finely chopped
4 × 15 ml spoons/4
   tablespoons chicken stock or
   water
275 g/10 oz frozen peas,
   thawed
50 g/2 oz proscuitto, cut into
   thin strips
salt
freshly ground black pepper

AMERICAN
2 tablespoons butter
1 small onion, finely chopped
¼ cup chicken bouillon or
   water
2 cups frozen peas, thawed
2 oz proscuitto, cut into thin
   strips
salt
freshly ground black pepper

Melt the butter in a saucepan and sauté the onion very gently for 5 minutes until soft. Add the stock (bouillon) and peas, bring to the boil, cover and simmer for 5 minutes. Add the proscuitto and cook, uncovered, stirring frequently, until the liquid is absorbed. Adjust the seasoning, transfer to a warmed serving dish, and serve immediately.
SERVES 4

Peas with Prosciutto

COURGETTE (ZUCCHINI) AND ANCHOVY SALAD

METRIC/IMPERIAL	AMERICAN
1 × 15 ml spoon/1 tablespoon olive oil	1 tablespoon olive oil
450 g/1 lb courgettes, sliced	1 lb zucchini, sliced
6 spring onions, chopped	6 scallions, chopped
150 ml/¼ pint chicken stock	⅔ cup chicken bouillon
1 × 50 g/1¾ oz can anchovy fillets	1 × 2 oz can anchovy fillets
2 × 15 ml spoons/2 tablespoons wine vinegar	2 tablespoons wine vinegar
1 × 5 ml spoon/1 teaspoon sugar	1 teaspoon sugar
1 clove garlic, crushed	1 clove garlic, crushed
freshly ground black pepper	freshly ground black pepper

Heat the oil in a frying pan. Add the sliced courgettes (zucchini) and spring onions (scallions) and sauté over moderate heat for 5 minutes. Add the stock, cover and simmer for 5 minutes, then drain.

Drain the anchovies, retaining the oil, and chop finely. Mix the vinegar, sugar and garlic with the anchovy oil and add pepper to taste. Toss the courgettes and anchovies in the dressing, place in a glass dish and chill before serving.

SERVES 4

Peperonata

NAPOLETANA FLAN

METRIC/IMPERIAL	AMERICAN
Pastry:	Dough:
100 g/4 oz plain flour	1 cup all-purpose flour
salt	salt
500 g/2 oz margarine	¼ cup margarine
2 × 15 ml spoons/2 tablespoons water	2 tablespoons water
Filling:	Filling:
25 g/1 oz butter	2 tablespoons butter
1 clove garlic, crushed	1 clove garlic, crushed
25 g/1 oz plain flour	¼ cup all-purpose flour
150 ml/¼ pint chicken stock	⅔ cup chicken bouillon
1 × 227 g/8 oz can tomatoes, drained	1 × 8 oz can tomatoes, drained
freshly ground black pepper	freshly ground black pepper
100 g/4 oz Mozarella or Bel Paese cheese, thinly sliced	¼ lb Mozarella or Bel Paese cheese, thinly sliced
To garnish:	To garnish:
1 × 50 g/1¾ oz can anchovy fillets, drained	1 × 2 oz anchovy fillets, drained
sliced stuffed olives	sliced stuffed olives

Sieve the flour and salt into a bowl and rub (cut) in the margarine until the mixture resembles fine breadcrumbs. Add enough water to make a stiff dough. Roll out the dough on a lightly floured surface and use to line a 20 cm/8 inch flan dish. Prick the base with a fork and line with baking beans. Place in a preheated hot oven (220°C/425°F, Gas Mark 7) and cook for 15 to 20 minutes. Remove beans and leave to cool.

Melt the butter in a pan and lightly sauté the garlic. Add the flour and cook for 1 minute, stirring. Remove from the heat and gradually stir in the stock (bouillon). Return to the heat, bring to the boil, stirring, and continue to cook for 2 minutes. Add the tomatoes and salt and pepper to taste. Mix well and turn into the flan case. Arrange the sliced cheese on top and garnish with anchovy fillets and olives.

Place the flan in a preheated moderately hot oven (200°C/400°F, Gas Mark 6) and cook for about 20 minutes until the cheese has melted. Serve immediately.

SERVES 4

PEPERONATA

METRIC/IMPERIAL
15 g/½ oz butter
2 × 15 ml spoons/2
   tablespoons oil
1 medium onion, finely
   chopped
4 red peppers, seeded and cut
   into strips
6 tomatoes, peeled, quartered
   and seeded
1 × 5 ml spoon/1 teaspoon
   sugar
salt
freshly ground black pepper
2 × 15 ml spoons/2
   tablespoons chopped parsley
   to garnish

AMERICAN
1 tablespoon butter
2 tablespoons oil
1 medium onion, finely
   chopped
4 red peppers, seeded and cut
   into strips
6 tomatoes, skinned,
   quartered and seeded
1 teaspoon sugar
salt
freshly ground black pepper
2 tablespoons chopped parsley
   to garnish

Heat the butter and oil in a saucepan, add the onion and
sauté for 5 minutes until soft. Add the peppers, cover and
simmer very gently for 15 minutes. Add the tomatoes and
sugar and salt and pepper to taste. Cover and simmer gently
for a further 15 minutes or until the vegetables form a thick
purée. Remove from the heat and adjust the seasoning.
Transfer to a warm serving dish, garnish with the chopped
parsley and serve immediately.
SERVES 4

ASPARAGUS MILANESE

METRIC/IMPERIAL
1 kg/2 lb asparagus
salt
50 g/2 oz butter
4 eggs
freshly ground black pepper
50 g/2 oz grated Parmesan
   cheese to garnish

AMERICAN
2 lb asparagus
salt
¼ cup butter
4 eggs
freshly ground black pepper
½ cup grated Parmesan
   cheese to garnish

Scrape the lower part of the asparagus stems with a sharp
knife, wash, then tie tightly together in small bundles.
Stand the asparagus upright in a pan of boiling salted water
so that the tips emerge just above water level. Cook for
about 20 minutes or until the tips are soft to the touch.
Drain, untie, and place in 4 individual warm serving
dishes. Keep hot.
Melt half the butter in a large frying pan (skillet) and cook
until it turns brown. Break the eggs into the pan and
sprinkle with salt and pepper. Cook until the egg whites
have set. Place one egg on each dish of asparagus. Melt the
remaining butter and pour over the asparagus. Sprinkle
with Parmesan and serve immediately.
SERVES 4

FRENCH (GREEN) BEANS IN GARLIC SAUCE

METRIC/IMPERIAL	AMERICAN
3 × 15 ml spoons/3 tablespoons olive oil	3 tablespoons olive oil
2 cloves garlic, crushed	2 cloves garlic, crushed
1 large ripe tomato, peeled and chopped	1 large ripe tomato, skinned and chopped
450 g/1 lb French beans, halved	1 lb green beans, halved
salt	salt
freshly ground black pepper	freshly ground black pepper

Heat the oil in a large saucepan, add the garlic and sauté gently until browned. Stir in the tomato, then add the beans. Add enough water to barely cover the beans, then add salt and pepper to taste and bring to the boil. Lower the heat, cover and simmer for 20 to 25 minutes until the beans are tender. Remove the lid 5 minutes before the end of cooking time and increase the heat to reduce the cooking liquid slightly. Transfer to a warm serving dish and serve immediately, or cold.

SERVES 4

BEANS WITH TUNA

METRIC/IMPERIAL	AMERICAN
175 g/6 oz dried haricot beans, soaked overnight in water	1 cup less 2 tablespoons dried navy beans, soaked overnight in water
1 small onion, thinly sliced	1 small onion, thinly sliced
olive oil for dressing	olive oil for dressing
salt	salt
freshly ground black pepper	freshly ground black pepper
1 × 198 g/7 oz can tuna, flaked	1 × 7 oz can tuna, flaked
chopped parsley to garnish	chopped parsley to garnish

Drain the beans, place in a saucepan and cover with fresh cold water. Bring to the boil, cover and simmer for 2½ to 3 hours, until tender. Drain and while still hot mix with the onion, olive oil and salt and pepper to taste. When cold, spoon into individual serving bowls. Stir in the flaked tuna and sprinkle with parsley. Serve immediately.

SERVES 4

FENNEL WITH BUTTER AND CHEESE

METRIC/IMPERIAL	AMERICAN
4 bulbs fennel	4 bulbs fennel
1 × 15 ml spoon/1 tablespoon olive oil	1 tablespoon olive oil
1 clove garlic, crushed	1 clove garlic, crushed
1 slice of lemon	1 slice of lemon
salt	salt
25 g/1 oz butter, melted	2 tablespoons butter, melted
2 × 15 ml spoons/2 tablespoons grated Parmesan cheese	2 tablespoons grated Parmesan cheese
freshly ground black pepper	freshly ground black pepper

Trim the top shoots and bases of the fennel and use a potato peeler to peel off any discoloured parts. Wash and cut into segments.

Put into a saucepan and cover with boiling water. Add the oil, garlic, lemon and salt. Bring to the boil, cover and simmer for 20 minutes or until just tender. Drain well. Pour the melted butter in a shallow flameproof dish. Add the fennel and toss to coat in butter. Sprinkle with cheese and pepper. Place under a preheated hot grill (broiler) and cook until browned. Serve immediately.

SERVES 4

POTATO CAKE

METRIC/IMPERIAL	AMERICAN
450 g/1 lb potatoes, peeled	1 lb potatoes, peeled
100 g/4 oz plain flour	1 cup all-purpose flour
salt	salt
freshly ground black pepper	freshly ground black pepper
3 eggs, beaten	3 eggs, beaten
4 × 15 ml spoons/4 tablespoons olive oil	¼ cup olive oil

Grate the potato into a bowl. Sieve in the flour and season with salt and pepper. Stir well, then mix in the eggs to form a soft, pliable dough.

Heat the oil in a frying pan (skillet), add the mixture and level. Sauté for about 7 minutes on each side until golden brown. Turn onto a warm serving dish and serve immediately.

SERVES 6

Beans with Tuna; Fennel with Butter and Cheese

CAKES AND DESSERTS

EASTER DOVE BREAD

METRIC/IMPERIAL
15 g/½ oz fresh yeast, or
    2 × 5 ml spoons/2
    teaspoons dried yeast and
    1 × 5 ml spoon/1 teaspoon
    caster sugar
150 ml/¼ pint warm milk
1 egg, beaten
1 × 5 ml spoon/1 teaspoon
    vanilla essence
275 g/10 oz strong plain white
    flour
1 × 5 ml spoon/1 teaspoon
    caster sugar
salt
grated rind of ½ lemon
25 g/1 oz butter
Glaze:
1 egg white, lightly beaten
1 × 15 ml spoon/1 tablespoon
    caster sugar

AMERICAN
½ cake compressed yeast, or 2
    teaspoons dried yeast and 1
    teaspoon sugar
⅔ cup warm milk
1 egg, beaten
1 teaspoon vanilla
2½ cups strong all-purpose
    flour
1 teaspoon sugar
salt
grated zest of ½ lemon
2 tablespoons butter
Glaze:
1 egg white, lightly beaten
1 tablespoon sugar

Blend the fresh yeast into the milk or dissolve the sugar in the milk and sprinkle on the dried yeast. Leave in a warm place for about 10 minutes or until frothy. Beat in the egg and vanilla.

In a large bowl, combine the flour, sugar, salt and grated lemon rind (zest). Rub (cut) in the butter. Beat the yeast liquid into the flour to form a firm dough. Turn onto a lightly floured surface and knead for 10 minutes until the dough is firm and no longer sticky. Place in a large bowl and cover with lightly oiled plastic wrap. Leave to rise in a warm place for 1 hour until double in size and springy to the touch.

Remove plastic wrap. Turn dough onto a lightly floured surface and knead for 2 minutes until smooth. Divide dough in half. Roll out one piece into an oval measuring 25 × 5 cm/10 × 2 inches. Place on a greased baking sheet and flatten out ends of oval. Roll remaining dough into a triangle measuring 13 cm/5 inch at the base and 25 cm/10 inch at each side. Arrange the triangle over the oval of dough to form a cross shape. Pinch the dough triangle just above and below the oval to form the head and body of the 'dove'. Elongate the tip of the triangle to form the beak. With a knife, score the tail and wings to look like feathers. Cover with lightly oiled plastic wrap and leave in a warm place until bread has increased in size slightly.

Uncover 'dove', and brush with egg white. Sprinkle sugar over wings and tail. Place in a preheated moderate oven (160°C/325°F, Gas Mark 3) and bake for 50 to 55 minutes until browned. Cool on a wire rack. Serve warm with butter.
SERVES 8 TO 10

PANETTONE

METRIC/IMPERIAL
50 g/2 oz caster sugar
25 g/1 oz fresh yeast
150 ml/¼ pint lukewarm
    water
3 egg yolks
salt
400 g/14 oz strong plain white
    flour
100 g/4 oz butter, softened
50 g/2 oz sultanas
50 g/2 oz seedless raisins
50 g/2 oz chopped mixed peel
25 g/1 oz butter, melted

AMERICAN
¼ cup sugar
1 cake compressed yeast
⅔ cup lukewarm water
3 egg yolks
salt
3½ cups strong all-purpose
    white flour
½ cup soft butter
⅔ cup raisins
⅓ cup chopped candied peel
2 tablespoons melted butter

Stir 1 × 5 ml spoon/1 teaspoon of the sugar and all of the yeast into the water. Leave for about 10 minutes or until frothy.

Beat the egg yolks and stir in the yeast mixture, salt and remaining sugar. Beat in 225 g/8 oz (2 cups) of the flour and then gradually beat in the softened butter, a little at a time. Knead in the remaining flour.

Turn the dough onto a lightly floured surface and knead well until the dough is firm and elastic. Place in a lightly oiled polythene bag and leave in a warm place until doubled in size. Turn dough out onto a floured surface and knead in the sultanas and seedless raisins (raisins) and peel. Continue kneading until the fruit is evenly distributed. Place the dough in a greased 18 cm/7 inch round cake tin (pan). Cover with oiled plastic wrap. Leave in a warm place until dough has risen to the top of the tin (pan).

Remove plastic wrap. Brush with some of the melted butter. Place in a preheated moderately hot oven (200°C/400°F, Gas Mark 6) and bake for 20 minutes. Reduce oven temperature to moderate (180°C/350°F, Gas Mark 4) and cook for a further 35 to 45 minutes. Remove from the tin (pan) and brush top and sides with remaining melted butter. Serve warm or cold cut into thin wedges.
SERVES 10

Neapolitan Curd Tart

NEAPOLITAN CURD TART

METRIC/IMPERIAL	AMERICAN
Pasta Frolla:	Pasta frolla:
225 g/8 oz plain flour	2 cups all-purpose flour
salt	salt
75 g/3 oz caster sugar	6 tablespoons sugar
100 g/4 oz butter, softened	½ cup butter, softened
finely grated rind of ½ lemon	finely grated rind of ½ lemon
2 egg yolks	2 egg yolks
Curd filling:	Curd filling:
350 g/12 oz Ricotta or curd cheese	1½ cups Ricotta or curd cheese
75 g/3 oz caster sugar	6 tablespoons sugar
3 eggs, well beaten	3 eggs, well beaten
50 g/2 oz blanched almonds, finely chopped	½ cup finely chopped blanched almonds
75 g/3 oz chopped mixed peel	½ cup chopped candied peel
finely grated rind of ½ lemon	finely grated rind of ½ lemon
finely grated rind of ½ orange	finely grated rind of ½ orange
½ × 2.5 ml spoon/¼ teaspoon vanilla essence	¼ teaspoon vanilla
icing sugar for dusting	confectioners' sugar for dusting

Sieve the flour, salt and sugar together in a heap on a work surface and make a well in the centre. Put the butter, lemon rind and egg yolks into the well. With the fingertips, gradually draw the flour into the centre and mix all the ingredients to a firm, smooth dough. Wrap the pastry in foil and chill in the refrigerator for 1 hour.

To make the filling: rub the cheese through the sieve (strainer) into a basin and beat in the sugar. Gradually beat in the eggs, followed by all the remaining ingredients except the icing (confectioners') sugar. Mix well.

Roll out the pastry (dough) thinly on a lightly floured surface and use to line an 18–20 cm/7–8 inch flan ring, reserving the trimmings for the decoration. Fill the flan with the cheese mixture and smooth the surface. Roll out the trimmings; with a fluted roller cut into thin 1 cm/½ inch wide strips and use to make a criss-cross pattern over the top of the flan.

Place in the centre of a preheated moderate oven (180°C/350°F, Gas Mark 4) and bake for 45 minutes. Cool on a wire rack. Serve cold, dusted with sugar.
SERVES 6

SICILIAN CAKE

METRIC/IMPERIAL	AMERICAN
Cake:	Cake:
225 g/8 oz soft margarine	1 cup soft margarine
225 g/8 oz caster sugar	1 cup sugar
4 eggs	4 eggs
225 g/8 oz self-raising flour, sifted with 2 × 5 ml spoons/ 2 teaspoons baking powder	2 cups self-rising flour, sifted with 2 teaspoons baking powder
grated rind of 2 oranges or 2 lemons	grated rind of 2 oranges or 2 lemons
Biscuits:	Cookies:
50 g/2 oz soft margarine	¼ cup soft margarine
75 g/3 oz plain flour	¾ cup all-purpose flour
25 g/1 oz sifted icing sugar	¼ cup sifted confectioners' sugar
Icing:	Frosting:
2 egg whites	2 egg whites
450 g/1 lb sifted icing sugar	3½ cups sifted confectioners' sugar

Grease and base line a 25 cm/10 inch square cake tin (pan). Place all the ingredients in a bowl and beat with a wooden spoon for 2 to 3 minutes until well mixed. Turn the mixture into the tin (pan). Place in a preheated moderate oven (160°C/325°F, Gas Mark 3) and bake for 35 to 45 minutes. Turn the cake onto a wire rack to cool and remove paper.

To make the biscuits (cookies): mix the margarine, flour and icing (confectioners') sugar in a bowl until the mixture forms a ball. Roll out thinly and cut out about 40 biscuits (cookies) with a heart-shaped cutter. Arrange on a lightly greased baking sheet. Place in a preheated moderate oven (180°C/350°F, Gas Mark 4) and bake for about 10 minutes. Transfer to a wire rack to cool.

To make the icing (frosting): beat the egg whites and sugar together until smooth. Using a piping (pastry) bag fitted with a plain writing nozzle (tip) pipe a lacy pattern on the top and sides of the cake and the tops of the biscuits (cookies). Place the cake on a large plate and arrange the biscuits (cookies) around the sides.

MAKES ONE 25 cm/10 inch square cake

CASSATA

METRIC/IMPERIAL	AMERICAN
600 ml/1 pint water	2½ cups water
150 g/5 oz dried skimmed milk powder	1⅔ cups dried skimmed milk powder
3 eggs	3 eggs
150 g/5 oz caster sugar	⅔ cup sugar
1 × 5 ml spoon/1 teaspoon vanilla essence	1 teaspoon vanilla
75 g/3 oz plain chocolate	3 oz semi-sweet chocolate
50 g/2 oz glacé cherries	¼ cup glacé cherries
25 g/1 oz mixed dried fruit	3 tablespoons mixed dried fruit
2 × 15 ml spoons/2 tablespoons sherry	2 tablespoons sherry

Whisk the water with the dried milk powder in a double boiler. Add the eggs, sugar and vanilla. Heat the custard gently, stirring continuously, until it is thick enough to coat the back of a wooden spoon; do not boil. Divide the custard into 2 separate freezer trays.

Shave off some large curls of chocolate and reserve.

Break the remaining chocolate into one of the freezer trays of hot custard and stir until melted. Allow to cool, then place the freezer trays in the freezer for about 1 hour or until the custard begins to thicken.

Meanwhile, chop the cherries and soak them with the dried fruit in the sherry.

Whisk both portions of half-frozen ice cream separately. Stir the fruit into the vanilla ice cream and return to the freezer. Measure half the chocolate ice cream into a 750 ml/ 1¼ pint (3 cup) loaf tin (pan). Level the surface and re-freeze. Keep the rest of the chocolate mixture cold. When the chocolate ice cream is sufficiently frozen, add the vanilla layer then finally the remainder of the chocolate ice cream. Leave to freeze hard.

To turn out, dip the pan quickly in hot water and invert onto a plate. Decorate with chocolate curls and cut into slices.

SERVES 8

SIENA CAKE

METRIC/IMPERIAL	AMERICAN
75 g/3 oz hazelnuts, toasted and coarsely chopped	½ cup filberts, toasted and coarsely chopped
75 g/3 oz blanched almonds, coarsely chopped	½ cup coarsely chopped blanched almonds
175 g/6 oz chopped mixed peel	1 cup finely chopped candied peel
25 g/1 oz cocoa powder	¼ cup unsweetened cocoa powder
50 g/2 oz plain flour	½ cup all-purpose flour
1 × 2.5 ml spoon/½ teaspoon ground cinnamon	½ teaspoon ground cinnamon
½ × 2.5 ml spoon/¼ teaspoon mixed spice	¼ teaspoon ground allspice
100 g/4 oz caster sugar	½ cup sugar
100 g/4 oz honey	⅓ cup honey
Topping:	Topping:
2 × 15 ml spoons/2 tablespoons icing sugar	2 tablespoons confectioners' sugar
1 × 5 ml spoon/1 teaspoon ground cinnamon	1 teaspoon ground cinnamon

Line a 20 cm/8 inch flan ring (pie pan) with buttered greaseproof (waxed) paper. Put the nuts, peel, cocoa, flour, cinnamon and spice into a mixing bowl and stir well.

Put the sugar and honey into a small saucepan, heat slowly until the sugar dissolves, then boil gently until a sugar thermometer registers 115°C/240°F, or until a little of the mixture dropped into a cup of cold water forms a soft ball. Take off the heat immediately, add the nut mixture and stir until well mixed.

Turn into the prepared flan ring (pie pan) and spread flat, making sure the mixture is not more than 1 cm/½ inch thick. Place in a preheated cool oven (150°C/300°F, Gas Mark 2) and bake for 30 to 35 minutes.

Allow to cool, then peel off the paper and sprinkle the top thickly with the icing (confectioners') sugar sifted with the cinnamon. Serve cut into small wedges.

MAKES ONE 20 cm/8 inch cake

Sicilian Gateau

SICILIAN GATEAU

METRIC/IMPERIAL
Cake:
4 eggs, separated
150 g/5 oz caster sugar
finely grated rind of ½ lemon
75 g/3 oz plain flour
25 g/1 oz cornflour
2 × 15 ml spoons/2
  tablespoons warm water
Filling and topping:
750 g/1½ lb Ricotta or curd
  cheese
175 g/6 oz caster sugar
5–6 × 15 ml spoons/5–6
  tablespoons orange liqueur
50 g/2 oz plain chocolate,
  finely chopped
75 g/3 oz chopped mixed peel
To decorate:
glacé fruits (optional)
strips of candied peel
coarsely grated chocolate

AMERICAN
Cake:
4 eggs, separated
⅔ cup sugar
finely grated rind of ½ lemon
¾ cup all-purpose flour
¼ cup cornstarch
2 tablespoons warm water
Filling and topping:
3 cups Ricotta or curd cheese
¾ cup sugar
5–6 tablespoons orange
  liqueur
2 squares semi-sweet
  chocolate, finely chopped
½ cup finely chopped candied
  peel
To decorate:
candied fruits (optional)
strips of candied peel
coarsely grated chocolate

First, make the cake: grease and flour a deep 23 cm/9 inch round cake tin (pan). Put the egg yolks, sugar and lemon rind into a large mixing bowl and beat until pale. Lightly fold in flour and cornflour (cornstarch), a little at a time, then add the water. Whisk the egg whites until stiff but not dry and fold into the cake mixture very lightly, but thoroughly.

Turn the mixture into the prepared tin (pan). Place in a preheated moderate oven (180°C/350°F, Gas Mark 4) and bake for 45 to 50 minutes until firm to the touch. Cool on a wire rack.

To make the filling and topping: press the cheese through a sieve (strainer) into a bowl, add the sugar and 2 × 15 ml spoons/2 tablespoons liqueur and beat until light and fluffy. Put half of this mixture into the refrigerator to chill for the topping. Add the chocolate and peel to the remainder and mix well.

Cut the cake horizontally into 3 layers. Place one layer on a serving dish, sprinkle with liqueur and spread with half of the filling. Cover with a second layer of sponge, sprinkle with liqueur and spread with the rest of the filling. Place the remaining layer of sponge on top. Press the layers together firmly and chill the cake in the refrigerator.

One hour before serving, spread the topping evenly over the top and sides of the cake. Decorate with glacé (candied) fruits if using, and peel. Sprinkle the top with coarsely grated chocolate.
SERVES 8 TO 10

LITTLE CHEESECAKES

METRIC/IMPERIAL	AMERICAN
Pastry:	Dough:
450 g/1 lb plain flour	4 cups all-purpose flour
4 eggs	4 eggs
2 × 15 ml spoons/2 tablespoons olive oil	2 tablespoons olive oil
salt	salt
Filling:	Filling:
250 g/9 oz grated Pecorino cheese	2 cups grated Pecorino cheese
25 g/1 oz sugar	2 tablespoons sugar
finely grated rind and juice of ½ lemon	finely grated zest and juice of ½ lemon
4 egg yolks	4 egg yolks

Sieve the flour onto a work surface and make a well in the centre. Add 3 eggs, the oil and salt and mix together to form a soft dough, adding lukewarm water if necessary.

Knead the dough until smooth and pliable. Shape into a ball, cover and chill in the refrigerator for 30 minutes.

Meanwhile, prepare the filling: place the cheese, sugar, lemon rind (zest) and juice and the egg yolks in a bowl and mix thoroughly. Roll out the dough on a lightly floured surface to 5 mm/¼ inch thickness. Cut into 7.5 cm/3 inch circles. Put a little of the filling in the middle of each circle, then fold the dough over the filling to form half-moon shapes. Moisten the edges then press firmly to seal.

Beat the remaining egg and brush over each cake and place on an oiled baking sheet. Place in a preheated moderate oven (180°C/350°F, Gas Mark 4) and bake for 30 minutes or until puffed and golden. Serve immediately.

MAKES 15 TO 20

CHERRIES IN RED WINE

METRIC/IMPERIAL	AMERICAN
100 g/4 oz sugar	½ cup sugar
1 thin strip of orange rind	1 thin strip of orange zest
pinch of ground cinnamon	pinch of ground cinnamon
1 × 15 ml spoon/1 tablespoon redcurrant jelly	1 tablespoon redcurrant jelly
150 ml/¼ pint red wine	⅔ cup red wine
450 g/1 lb large black cherries, stoned	1 lb large bing cherries, pitted
butter for shallow frying	butter for shallow frying
4 thin small slices crustless bread	4 thin small slices crustless bread

Put the sugar, orange rind (zest), cinnamon, redcurrant jelly and wine into a saucepan. Heat gently until the sugar has dissolved, then boil for 1 minute. Add the cherries and simmer gently for 15 minutes.

Melt the butter in a large frying pan (skillet) and sauté the bread slices until golden on both sides. Drain and arrange in 4 shallow plates. Using a perforated spoon, drain the cherries and arrange on the bread slices.

Reduce the syrup by boiling rapidly for a few minutes, then strain over the cherries. Serve immediately.

SERVES 4

STUFFED BAKED PEACHES

METRIC/IMPERIAL	AMERICAN
4 large firm ripe peaches	4 large firm ripe peaches
50 g/2 oz fine sponge cake crumbs	1 cup fine sponge cake crumbs
50 g/2 oz ground almonds	½ cup ground almonds
50 g/2 oz caster sugar	¼ cup sugar
25 g/1 oz butter, softened	2 tablespoons butter, softened
juice of 1 lemon	juice of 1 lemon

Immerse the peaches in boiling water for a few seconds to loosen their skins, then drain and plunge into cold water. Peel, halve and remove the stones (seeds). Using a teaspoon, scoop enough flesh from each half to make a deep indentation for the stuffing. Chop the peach flesh.

Mix the peach flesh with the cake crumbs, nuts, sugar, butter and lemon juice to moisten. Pile the stuffing into the peach halves and smooth the top. Arange the peaches, side by side in a shallow buttered ovenproof dish. Place in a preheated moderate oven (180°C/350°F, Gas Mark 4) and bake for 30 to 35 minutes. Serve hot, warm or cold.

SERVES 4

SWEET PIZZA

METRIC/IMPERIAL	AMERICAN
Pastry:	Dough:
225 g/8 oz plain flour	2 cups all-purpose flour
salt	salt
100 g/4 oz margarine	½ cup margarine
cold water	cold water
Filling:	Filling:
4 × 15 ml spoons/4 tablespoons honey	4 tablespoons honey
50 g/2 oz chopped walnuts	½ cup chopped walnuts
1 × 5 ml spoon/1 teaspoon mixed spice	1 teaspoon ground allspice
50 g/2 oz chopped mixed peel	⅓ cup chopped candied peel
To finish:	To finish:
1 × 15 ml spoon/1 tablespoon warmed honey	1 tablespoon warmed honey
25 g/1 oz chopped walnuts	¼ cup chopped walnuts

Sieve the flour and salt into a bowl and rub (cut) in the margarine until the mixture resembles breadcrumbs. Add sufficient cold water to make a dough. Roll out the dough thinly on a lightly floured surface into a rectangle. Spread the honey over the dough and sprinkle with the walnuts, spice and peel. Roll up the dough into a long sausage shape.

Brush the roll with warmed honey and sprinkle with walnuts. Make cuts along the roll at 2.5 cm/1 inch intervals. Place in a preheated moderate oven (180°C/350°F, Gas Mark 4) and bake for 25 minutes. Serve warm or cold.

SERVES 4

Stuffed Baked Peaches; Cherries in Red Wine

CARAMELIZED ORANGES

METRIC/IMPERIAL	AMERICAN
6 large seedless oranges	6 large seedless oranges
225 g/8 oz sugar	1 cup sugar
300 ml/½ pint water	1⅓ cups water
1 × 15 ml spoon/1 tablespoon Arum or any orange liqueur (optional)	1 tablespoon Arum or any orange liqueur (optional)

Thinly pare the rind from one orange. Shred the rind finely and simmer in just enough water to cover, for 8 minutes or until tender. Drain. Using a serrated knife, peel the rind, pith and skin from the oranges.

Place the sugar and 150 ml/¼ pint (⅔ cup) of the water in a pan over low heat. Stir until completely dissolved, then boil for a few minutes until cloudy. Remove from the heat, add the oranges, 3 at a time, and spoon the syrup over them. Lift out and arrange in a serving dish.

Add the strips of rind to the remaining syrup and heat gently until the syrup begins to caramelize and turn pale gold. Quickly take the pan off the heat and stand in a bowl of warm water to stop further cooking. Put a little of the caramelized rind on top of each orange.

Add the remaining 150 ml/¼ pint (⅔ cup) water, and the orange liqueur if using, to the pan and heat, stirring, until the caramel dissolves. Leave until cold then pour over the oranges. Serve slightly chilled.

SERVES 6

COFFEE GRANITA

METRIC/IMPERIAL	AMERICAN
150 g/5 oz finely ground fresh coffee	2½ cups finely ground fresh coffee
75 g/3 oz caster sugar	6 tablespoons sugar
1 litre/1¾ pints boiling water	4¼ cups boiling water
To serve:	To serve:
whipped cream (optional)	whipped cream (optional)
finely ground coffee (optional)	finely ground coffee (optional)

Put the coffee and sugar into a warm earthenware jug and pour the boiling water over it. Cover and stand the jug in a saucepan of boiling water and leave to infuse for 30 minutes. Cool.

When cold, strain through a filter paper. Pour into a shallow tray and freeze, without stirring, until frozen to a granular but solid mush.

Scoop into 4 or 6 tall glasses, and serve either plain or topped with whipped cream and a sprinkling of coffee.

SERVES 4 TO 6

CREAM ICE

METRIC/IMPERIAL	AMERICAN
2 egg yolks	2 egg yolks
50 g/2 oz icing sugar, sifted	½ cup sifted confectioners' sugar
2 × 5 ml spoons/2 teaspoons vanilla essence	2 teaspoons vanilla
300 ml/½ pint double cream	1¼ cups heavy cream
2 × 15 ml spoons/2 tablespoons milk	2 tablespoons milk

Peach Water Ice; Coffee Granita

Put egg yolks and sugar into a double boiler and beat until thick and creamy. Remove from the heat. Continue beating the mixture until cool, then stir in the vanilla.

Pour the cream and milk into a chilled bowl and beat until lightly stiff. Gently fold in beaten yolks and sugar and then transfer to 1 or 2 ice cube trays, depending on size. Freeze for 45 minutes or until cream ice has frozen about 1 cm/½ inch around sides of tray. Turn into a chilled bowl, break up gently with a fork then stir until smooth. Return to washed and dried tray and freeze for 1½ to 2 hours or until firm.

SERVES 4

PEACH WATER ICE

METRIC/IMPERIAL	AMERICAN
100 g/4 oz sugar	½ cup sugar
150 ml/¼ pint water	⅔ cup water
4 large peaches	4 large peaches
juice of 1 lemon	juice of 1 lemon

Put the sugar and water into a small saucepan and heat gently until the sugar has completely dissolved, then boil without stirring, for 5 minutes. Leave until quite cold.

Immerse the peaches in boiling water for 1 minute, drain and remove skin and stones (seeds). Quickly purée the flesh in a blender. Immediately mix thoroughly with the lemon juice to prevent discolouration. Stir in the cold syrup, pour into a shallow freezer tray and freeze.

When partially frozen, turn into a bowl and whisk vigorously for a few minutes, then return to the tray and freeze until firm.

An hour before serving, transfer to the refrigerator to allow the ice to soften a little.

SERVES 4

TORTONI

METRIC/IMPERIAL	AMERICAN
1 egg white	1 egg white
300 ml/½ pint double cream	1¼ cups heavy cream
4 × 15 ml spoons/4 tablespoons icing sugar, sifted	½ cup confectioners' sugar, sifted
3 × 15 ml spoons/3 tablespoons brandy or liqueur	3 tablespoons brandy or liqueur
40 g/1½ oz flaked almonds, toasted	⅓ cup slivered almonds, toasted

Whisk the egg white until stiff. In another bowl, whisk the cream until beginning to thicken, then add half the sugar and half the brandy or liqueur and whisk until thick. Repeat with the remaining sugar and brandy. Fold in the egg white.

Spoon the mixture into 6 or 8 ice cream paper cases or freezerproof sundae glasses and top with the toasted almonds. Place in deep containers and cover loosely with foil so that the ices are covered but not flattened. Freeze for 3 hours.

About 30 minutes before serving, transfer from the freezer to the refrigerator to allow the ices to soften a little before serving.

SERVES 6 TO 8

HOT ZABAIONE

METRIC/IMPERIAL	AMERICAN
3 egg yolks	3 egg yolks
2 × 15 ml spoons/2 tablespoons caster sugar	2 tablespoons caster sugar
150 ml/¼ pint Marsala, Madeira or sweet sherry	⅔ cup Marsala, Madeira or sweet sherry

Put the egg yolks into a double boiler. Add the sugar and Marsala, Madeira or sweet sherry and whisk for about 8 minutes until thick and creamy. Serve immediately, in tall glasses.

SERVES 3

ALMOND SOUFFLÉ

METRIC/IMPERIAL	AMERICAN
Almond purée:	Almond purée:
75 g/3 oz flaked almonds	¾ cup slivered almonds
150 ml/¼ pint milk	⅔ cup milk
2 × 5 ml spoons/2 teaspoons caster sugar	2 teaspoons sugar
2 macaroons	2 macaroons
100 ml/3 fl oz pint Amaretto di Saronno	½ cup Amaretto di Saronno
sifted icing sugar to decorate	sifted confectioners' sugar to decorate
Soufflé:	Soufflé:
150 ml/¼ pint milk	⅔ cup milk
1 drop vanilla essence	1 drop vanilla
15 g/½ oz butter	1 tablespoon butter
25 g/1 oz strong plain white flour	¼ cup strong all-purpose white flour
3 egg yolks (1 to be kept separate)	3 egg yolks (1 to be kept separate)
4 egg whites	4 egg whites
25 g/1 oz caster sugar	2 tablespoons sugar

To make the almond purée: put the almonds, milk and sugar in a saucepan and simmer gently for 40 minutes. When cooked, cool slightly and blend in a blender, until the mixture is fine.

Grease and flour four 7.5 cm/3 inch individual soufflé dishes. Soak the macaroons with half the Amaretto and put one macaroon, cut into cubes, into each dish.

To prepare the soufflé: put two-thirds of the milk into a heavy pan with the vanilla and butter and bring to the boil. Remove from the heat and stir in the remaining milk, flour and one egg yolk. Heat again until the mixture becomes thick, and then whisk briskly. Add the 5 remaining egg yolks and cook for a further 2 minutes until the mixture begins to stiffen. Whisk the egg whites until stiff and whisk in the sugar.

Blend the soufflé mixture with the almond purée and remaining Amaretto. Carefully fold in the stiffly beaten egg whites. Spoon this mixture into the soufflé dishes. Place in a preheated hot oven (220°C/425°F, Gas Mark 7) and cook for 10 to 12 minutes. Dust with icing (confectioners') sugar and serve immediately.

SERVES 4

COLD ZABAIONE

METRIC/IMPERIAL	AMERICAN
75 g/3 oz sugar	6 tablespoons sugar
150 ml/¼ pint water	⅔ cup water
3 egg yolks	3 egg yolks
1 × 15 ml spoon/1 tablespoon Marsala, Madeira or sweet sherry	1 tablespoon Marsala, Madeira or sweet sherry
150 ml/¼ pint double cream, whipped	⅔ cup heavy cream, whipped

Place the sugar and water in a saucepan. Stir over low heat to dissolve the sugar. Boil until a thick syrup is formed. Gradually whisk the syrup into the egg yolks with the Marsala, Madeira or sweet sherry. Keep whisking until thick and creamy. Fold in the whipped cream and chill in the refrigerator for 1 hour. Serve in tall glasses.

SERVES 3

MONTE BIANCO

METRIC/IMPERIAL	AMERICAN
450 g/1 lb chestnuts	1 lb chestnuts
2 × 15 ml spoons/2 tablespoons milk	2 tablespoons milk
175 g/6 oz icing sugar, sifted	1⅓ cups confectioners' sugar, sifted
salt	salt
150 ml/¼ pint double cream	⅔ cup heavy cream
2 × 15 ml spoons/2 tablespoons brandy, rum or Strega liqueur	2 tablespoons brandy, rum or Strega liqueur

Cut a cross at the pointed end of each chestnut with a knife. Put them in a pan, cover with water, bring to the boil and simmer for 15 minutes. Drain and leave until cool enough to handle. While still quite hot, peel off the shells and inner skins.

Return the chestnuts to the pan, cover with cold water and bring to the boil. Simmer for 45 minutes or until soft. Drain and purée the chestnuts with the milk in a blender. Stir in the sugar and salt.

Pile the chestnut purée into a mound on a serving dish. Whip the cream with the brandy, rum or liqueur until thick but not stiff. Swirl lightly over the top of the mound, leaving the base uncovered.

Alternatively, spoon the chestnut purée into individual glasses and swirl the flavoured whipped cream on top. Serve immediately.

SERVES 4

Almond Soufflé; Cold Zabaione

PIGNOLATA STRUFOLI

METRIC/IMPERIAL	AMERICAN
150 g/5 oz plain flour	1¼ cups all-purpose flour
salt	salt
2 eggs	2 eggs
oil for shallow frying	oil for shallow frying
100 g/4 oz caster sugar	½ cup sugar
7 × 15 ml spoons/7 tablespoons clear honey	7 tablespoons honey
25 g/1 oz flaked almonds	¼ cup slivered almonds

Sieve 100 g/4 oz (1 cup) flour and salt onto a board and make a well in the centre. Break the eggs into the well and knead, gradually adding remaining flour until mixture has formed a medium soft dough. Roll out dough on a lightly floured surface to 5 mm/¼ inch thick. Cut into 5 mm/¼ inch wide strips. Twist two strands together and cut into pieces 1 cm/½ inch long.

Heat the oil and, when very hot, add the pieces of dough, a few at a time. Cook for 1 to 2 minutes, stirring. Remove from the oil and drain on kitchen paper towels.

Put the sugar and honey in a saucepan and cook, stirring over moderate heat for 5 minutes; do not boil. Add the cooked 'twists' to the mixture, stirring until they are completely covered with syrup. Arrange like two bunches of grapes on two plates. Decorate with almonds 'leaves'.

SERVES 8

FIG AND NUT PASTRIES

METRIC/IMPERIAL	AMERICAN
Pastry:	Dough:
400 g/14 oz plain flour	3½ cups all-purpose flour
150 g/5 oz caster sugar	⅔ cup sugar
150 g/5 oz butter, softened and cut into small pieces	⅔ cup butter, softened and cut into small pieces
3 eggs	3 eggs
1 egg yolk	1 egg yolk
salt	salt
Filling:	Filling:
300 g/11 oz dried figs	2 cups dried figs
150 g/5 oz shelled walnuts, ground	1¼ cups shelled walnuts, ground
150 g/5 oz blanched almonds, toasted and ground	1¼ cups blanched almonds, toasted and ground
100 g/4 oz seedless raisins, soaked in lukewarm water for 15 minutes and drained	⅔ cup seedless raisins, soaked in lukewarm water for 15 minutes and drained
200 g/7 oz marmalade	¾ cup marmalade
finely grated rind of 3 oranges	finely grated rind of 3 oranges
½ × 2.5 ml spoon/¼ teaspoon ground cloves	¼ teaspoon ground cloves
1 × 5 ml spoon/1 teaspoon ground cinnamon	1 teaspoon ground cinnamon

To make the pastry (dough): sieve the flour into a bowl, stir in the sugar, then make a well in the centre. Add the butter, 2 eggs, 1 egg yolk and salt. Work the ingredients together with the fingertips to form a soft dough, then knead well until smooth and elastic. Shape the dough into a ball, cover and chill in the refrigerator.

Cook the figs in boiling water for 10 minutes. Drain thoroughly, then chop. Place in a bowl with the remaining filling ingredients and mix thoroughly.

Roll out the dough on a lightly floured surface to 5 mm/¼ inch thickness. Cut into eight 10 cm/4 inch circles, using a pastry (cookie) cutter. Put a little filling in the middle of each circle, then fold the dough over the filling to form half-moon shapes. Moisten the edges then press firmly to seal. Make a few cuts in the surface of each pastry and place on a greased baking sheet. Beat remaining egg and brush over pastries. Place in a preheated moderate oven (160°C/325°F, Gas Mark 3) and bake for 25 to 30 minutes until puffed and golden. Serve immediately, or cold.

MAKES 8

ALMOND AND PINE NUT BISCUITS

METRIC/IMPERIAL	AMERICAN
75 g/3 oz ground almonds	¾ cup ground almonds
200 g/7 oz caster sugar	⅞ cup sugar
few drops vanilla essence	few drops vanilla essence
pinch of salt	pinch of salt
2 egg whites	2 egg whites
100 g/4 oz pine nuts roughly chopped	1 cup pine nuts, roughly chopped

Pound the almonds and half the sugar to a fine powder with a pestle and mortar or place in a blender for 1 minute on high speed. Turn into a large bowl and add the vanilla.

Add the salt to the egg whites and whisk until standing in soft peaks, then beat in the remaining sugar a little at a time. Fold the egg whites lightly but thoroughly into the almond mixture.

Spread the pine nuts on a board. Drop small spoonfuls of the almond mixture onto the nuts, rolling them gently until coated with nuts. Lightly butter two baking sheets and dust lightly with flour. Arrange the nut-coated pieces about 2.5 cm/1 inch apart on the baking sheets. Bake in a preheated moderately hot oven (200°C/400°F, Gas Mark 6) for about 10 minutes until golden.

MAKES 20 TO 24 BISCUITS

APPLE FRITTERS

METRIC/IMPERIAL	AMERICAN
50 g/2 oz butter, melted	¼ cup butter, melted
50 g/2 oz caster sugar	¼ cup sugar
150 ml/¼ pint milk	⅔ cup milk
50 g/2 oz plain flour	½ cup all-purpose flour
3 eggs, beaten	3 eggs, beaten
1 × 5 ml spoon/1 teaspoon dried yeast, dissolved in 2 × 5 ml spoons/2 teaspoons warm water	1 teaspoon active dry yeast, dissolved in 2 teaspoons warm water
8 dessert apples, peeled, cored and sliced into rounds	8 dessert apples, peeled, cored and sliced into rounds
vegetable oil for deep-frying	vegetable oil for deep-frying

Put the melted butter in a bowl with half the sugar, milk, flour, eggs and yeast. Beat to a smooth batter. Sprinkle the apple slices with the remaining sugar.

Heat the oil in a deep-fryer. Dip the apple slices a few at a time into the batter, then deep-fry in the hot oil until golden brown. Drain on kitchen paper towels and keep warm while frying the remainder. Serve immediately.

SERVES 6 TO 8

Nocciollette

NOCCIOLLETTE

METRIC/IMPERIAL	AMERICAN
100 g/4 oz butter	½ cup butter
40 g/1½ oz icing sugar	⅓ cup confectioners' sugar
1½ × 15 ml spoons/1½ tablespoons honey	1½ tablespoons honey
100 g/4 oz plain flour	1 cup all-purpose flour
75 g/3 oz hazelnuts, toasted and coarsely ground	½ cup filberts, toasted and coarsely ground
icing sugar for dusting.	confectioners' sugar for dusting

Cream the butter, sugar and honey together until light and fluffy, then stir in the flour and nuts, mixing to a smooth dough. With lightly floured hands, pinch off pieces of dough the size of walnuts and shape into ovals. Arrange these on greased baking sheets, 2.5 cm/1 inch apart.

Place in a preheated moderate oven (180°C/350°F, Gas Mark 4) and bake for about 15 minutes until firm. Cool slightly and roll in icing (confectioners') sugar.

MAKES ABOUT 24

AMARETTI

METRIC/IMPERIAL	AMERICAN
225 g/8 oz blanched almonds	2 cups blanched almonds
50 g/2 oz bitter almonds	1 cup bitter almonds
350 g/12 oz caster sugar	1½ cups superfine sugar
25 g/1 oz plain flour, sifted	¼ cup all-purpose flour, sifted
4 egg whites	4 egg whites
few drops of vanilla essence	few drops vanilla
½ × 2.5 ml spoon/¼ teaspoon grated lemon rind	¼ teaspoon grated lemon rind

Grind all the almonds together, using a pestle and mortar or food processor. Place in a bowl with all except 2 tablespoons of the sugar and all the flour; stir well to mix. Lightly whisk the egg whites, then add the vanilla and lemon rind. Add to the almond mixture gradually, until mixture is smooth and soft and holds its shape.

Place small spoonfuls of the mixture on a greased and floured baking sheet, spacing them well apart. Sprinkle with the remaining sugar. Place in a preheated moderate oven (180°C/350°F, Gas Mark 4) and bake for about 20 minutes or until lightly browned. Transfer to a wire tack to cool completely before serving.

MAKES 35 TO 40

ITALIAN INGREDIENTS

Pasta: Available in many different shapes and used in many different ways. They are all available dried in packets and many are now available from specialist delicatessens fresh. The small shapes can be used in soups and stews.

Rice: Italian recipes call for arboreo rice which is shorter and thicker than other types of rice and absorbs more water. It is essential for a good risotto.

Wine Vinegar: Salad dressing will not taste Italian unless made with wine vinegar. It is also used in many other recipes.

Olive Oil: The true taste of Italian salads and many other dishes can only be achieved with olive oil. As it is expensive, buy the strongest virgin oil and dilute with sunflower or groundnut oil.

Canned Peeled Tomatoes: Italian plum tomatoes have quite a different taste from English round tomatoes. Keep a couple of tins handy in the store cupboard as they are time-saving as well as delicious in stews and sauces.

Tomato Purée: Available in cans or tubes, tomato purée is highly concentrated and a teaspoonful is enough to add flavour to a sauce.

Parmesan Cheese: The sharpness of freshly grated Parmesan gives a wonderful flavour to pasta and sauces. Buy it by the piece and grate it yourself as ready-grated Parmesan available in packets and tubs does not taste the same.

Mozzarella Cheese: Used as a topping for pizzas and in salads. Should be kept in a bowl of water to retain its softness.

Ricotta: A creamy white cheese which must be eaten fresh. Used in savoury stuffings and sweets. Cottage cheese can be used as a substitute but does not have the same flavour.

Salami: Long dry-cured sausages of ground meat with fat and spices. Each area of Italy makes its own salami, but Milano is the best and available widely in this country. Slice thinly and add to antipasti or chop into sauces and stuffings.

Bresaola: Dry cured beef fillet, eaten raw as an antipasto in very thin slices.

Prosciutto: Delicately cured ham, also served wafer thin as an antipasto, often with melon or figs. The best comes from Parma or San Daniele.

Mortadella: Large, smooth-textured pork sausage containing fat and spices. Served sliced as an antipasto.

Pancetta: Salted raw belly of pork. This is used to give extra flavour to sauces and soups and can be used in stuffings. Pancetta can be bought sliced or in one piece.

Wine: Both red and white wines are used in Italian cooking. Barbera is a good red wine to use, and Orvieto, Soave or Frascati are excellent white wines. Marsala is used a great deal, especially in veal dishes and in the dessert Zabaione.

ITALIAN DELICATESSENS

Camisa
61 Old Compton Street,
London, W.1.
Tel: 01-437-7610

Luigi
Fulham Road,
London, S.W.10.
Tel: 01-352-7739

G.B. Fabrizi
289 Regents Park Road,
London, N.3.
Tel: 01-349-9422

Italian Delicatessen Store
33 Willesden Lane,
London, N.W.6.
Tel: 01-328-5072

King's Cross Continental Stores
26 Caledonian Road,
London, N.1.
Tel: 01-837-0201

Continental Specialities
St. Martin's Arcade,
The Bull Ring,
Birmingham.
Tel: 021-643-0869

C & T Licata & Son
36 Picton Street,
Montpelier,
Bristol.
Tel: 0272-47725

R & M Wines
66 Victoria Street,
Manchester.
Tel: 061-832-2601

Valvona & Crolla
19 Elm Row,
Edinburgh 7.
Tel: 031-556-6066

Graham O'Sullivan Ltd
11 Duke Street,
Dublin 2.
Tel: Dublin 716643

ACKNOWLEDGMENTS

The following colour photographs are by courtesy of:
Bryce Attwell: 2–5
Robert Golden: endpapers; 6–11; 14–63; 68–93
Paul Kemp: 67
John Lee & Rex Bamber: 65
Norman Nicholls: 12

INDEX

PDO 82-0727